the key to learni

SCALES AND ARPEGGIOS

for piano grades 1 to 5

A new method focusing on simultaneous finger patterns

Playing with hands together is EASY with this method

Jane Mann

Introduction

As a piano teacher with over 20 years' experience, many of my pupils struggled to learn scales and arpeggios. When playing with both hands together, fingering often became muddled, particularly on descending.

This book is the result of helping my pupils overcome the confusion. They now approach their scales and arpeggios with confidence, rapidly gaining accuracy throughout.

- There are **simple rules, or anchor points, which identify where LH and RH fingers play simultaneously** in each scale and arpeggio.
- Learning and applying these rules **fixes the finger coordination when playing both hands together**, making the learning process easier, quicker and more secure.

This scale and arpeggio method is organised into groups of finger patterns according to these rules.

There are five scale groups and three arpeggio groups based on traditional fingering.

For example:

- Group 1 contains 13 scales with the same rule:
- **'Both LH and RH 3rd fingers play together throughout'.**

Think of the rules and watch your hands. **It's easy!**

I could not conceive of teaching without this method – it is a valuable tool for ALL pianists.

Melodic minor scales are not included but have the same fingering as the harmonic minor scales, apart from the scales of Bb minor and F# minor.

Contents

ARPEGGIOS

CONTRARY MOTION SCALES

The Scales Groups

Group 1

C major	A minor	Ab major
G major	D minor	G# minor
D major	E minor	C# minor
A major	C minor	
E major	G minor	

Group 2

B major F# major Db major

Group 3

Eb major Bb major

Group 4

F major F minor

Group 5

B minor	Eb minor
Bb minor	F# minor

The Arpeggio Groups

Group 1

C major	A minor	B major
G major	D minor	B minor
D major	E minor	F# major
A major	C minor	Eb minor
E major	G minor	
F major	F minor	

Group 2

Db major	Ab major	Eb major
F# minor	C# minor	G# minor

Group 3

Bb major	Bb minor

How to Practise

1. Learn one octave with separate hands.

2. Learn two octaves, still with separate hands.

3. Play one octave with both hands together, gradually increasing your speed. Repeat this until your fingering becomes automatic.

4. Continue to play two octaves with separate hands.

5. Now play two octaves with both hands together, slowly at first, then increase your speed.

Repetition is required until your fingers play automatically.

Play everything **at least five times** each practice.

Play the TONIC CHORD.

Notice the raised seventh note in minor scales.

Tips:

Test yourself on the finger rule before starting each scale.

Watch continually for the correct finger patterns.

Listen for an even tone and clear legato sound.

Scales

Group 1

RULE: 3rd fingers play together

C major	A minor	Ab major
G major	D minor	G# minor
D major	E minor	C# minor
A major	C minor	
E major	G minor	

Tones and Semitones in scales:-

Major	T	T	S	T	T	T	S
Harmonic Minor	T	S	T	T	S	2	S

(Jump over 2 notes)

Tips:

- Keeping a careful eye on the tones and semitones rule is helpful.
- Remember to play the tonic chord before each scale.
- The **middle note** of a **minor chord** is the **related major keynote.**

Group 1

C Major Scale

RH PLAY THE CHORD

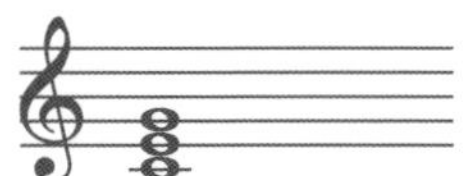

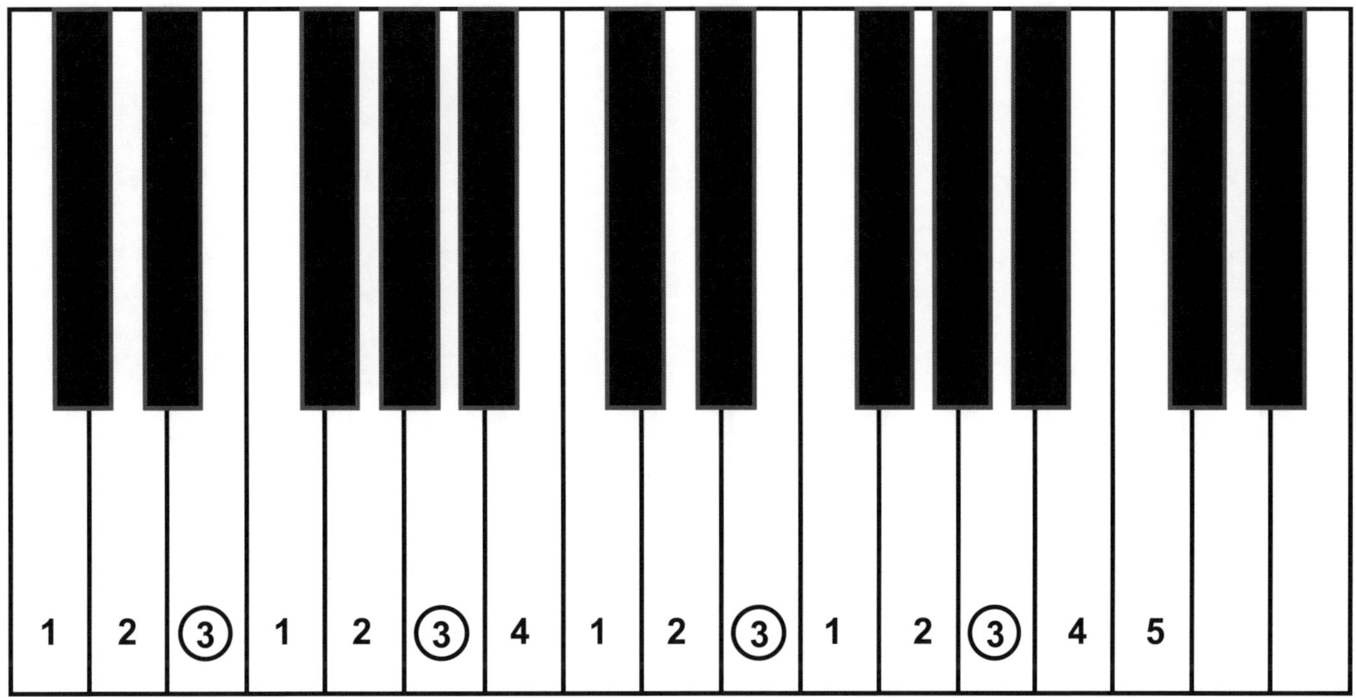

3rd fingers play together

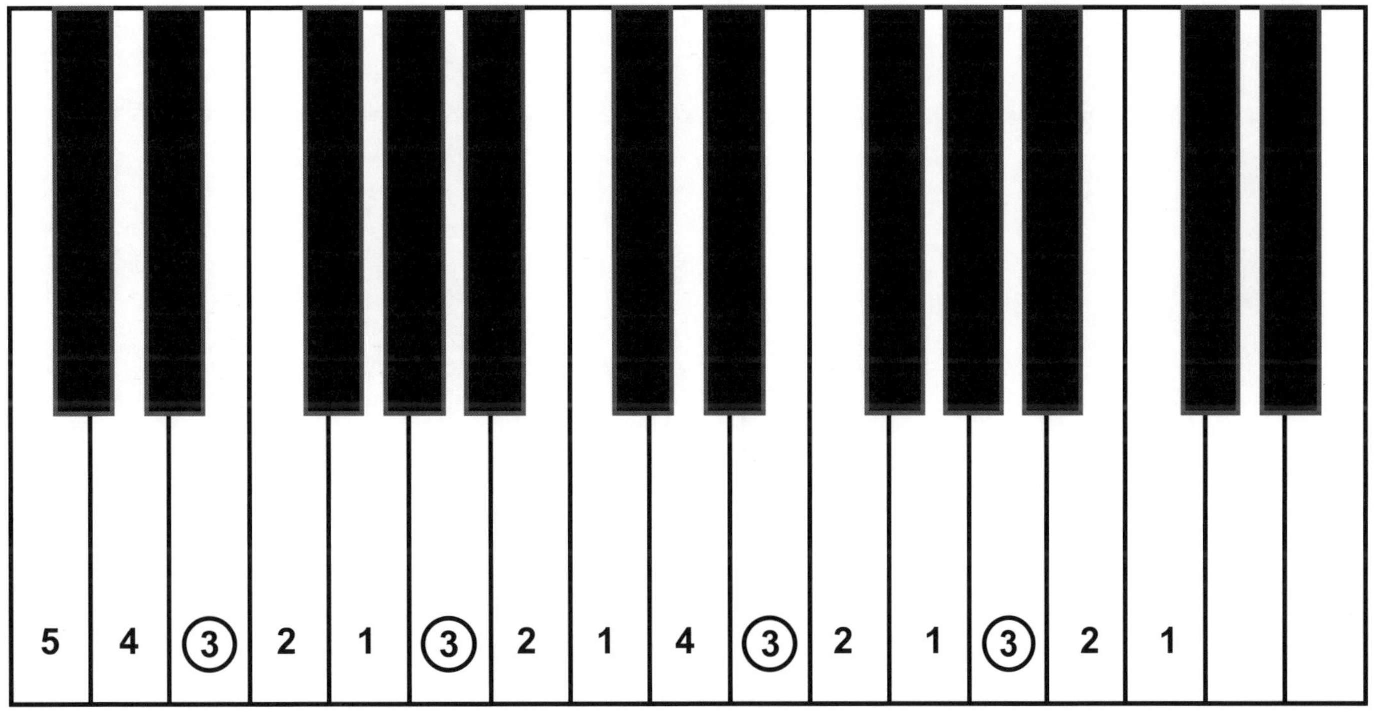

Group 1

C Major Scale

LH PLAY THE CHORD

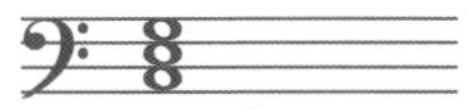

Group 1

G Major Scale

RH PLAY THE CHORD

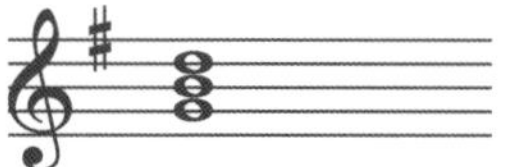

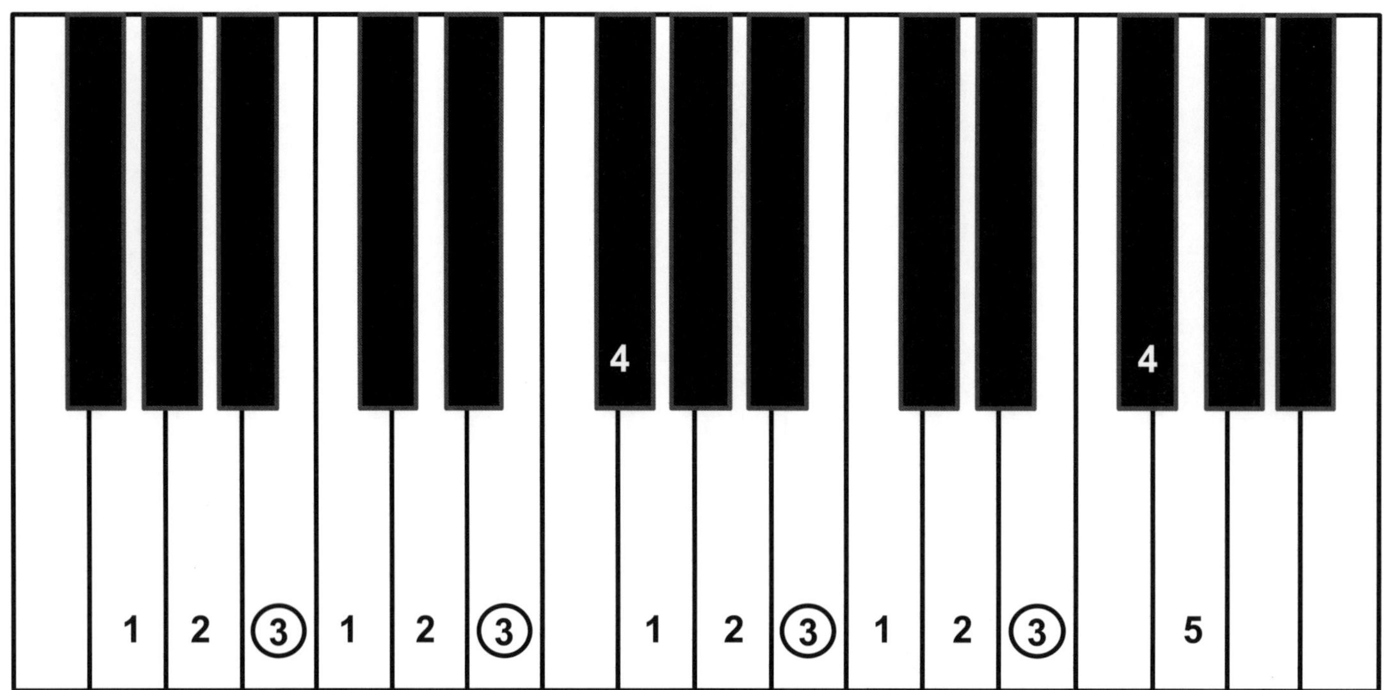

3rd fingers play together

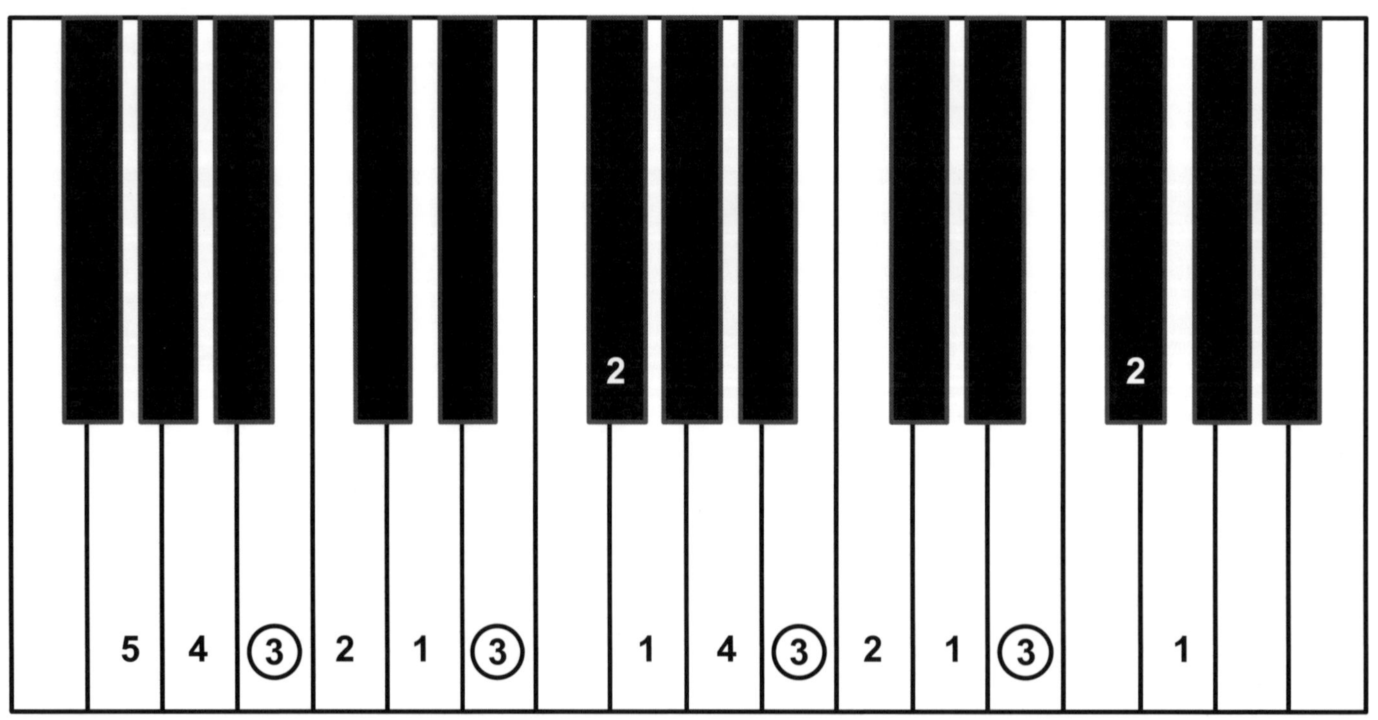

Group 1

G Major Scale

LH PLAY THE CHORD

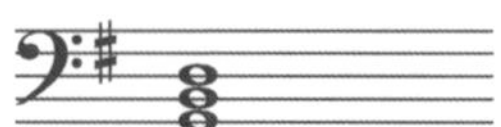

Group 1
D Major Scale
RH PLAY THE CHORD

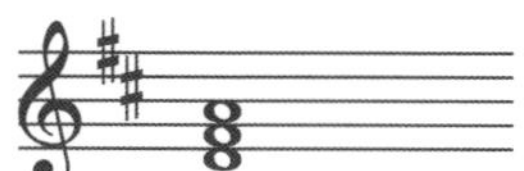

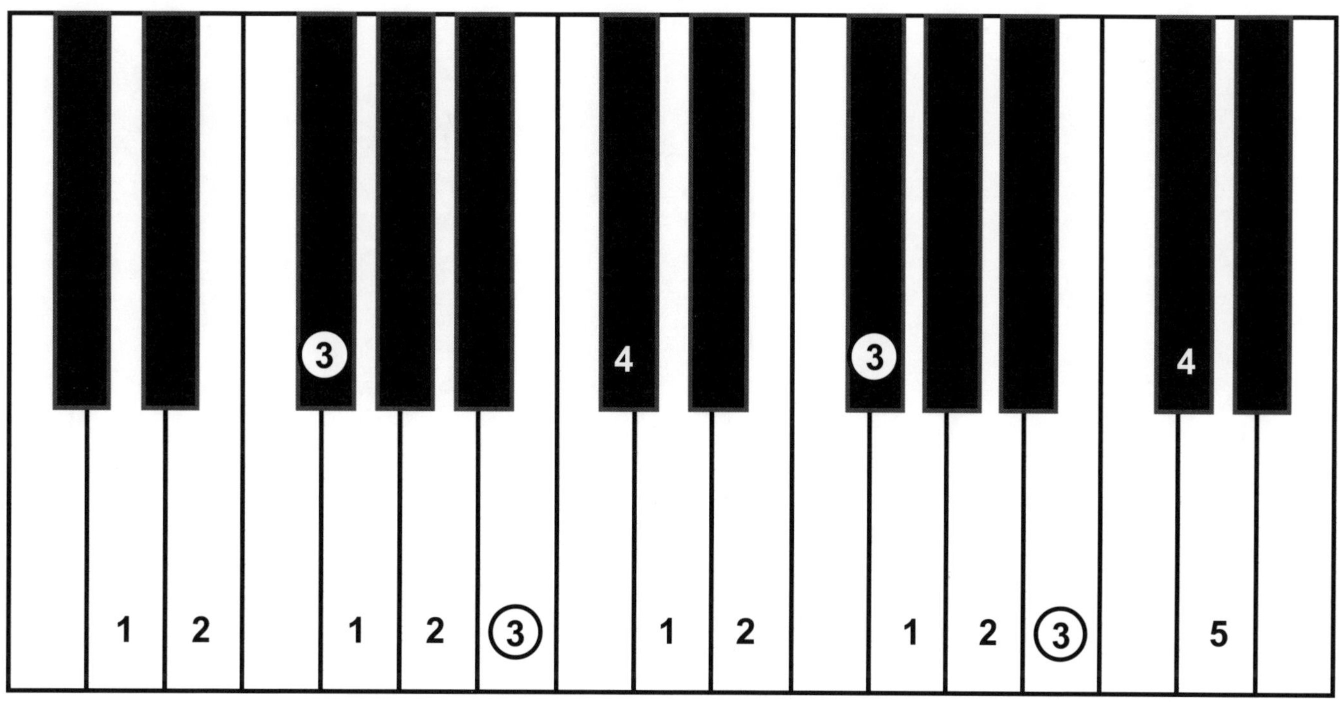

3rd fingers play together

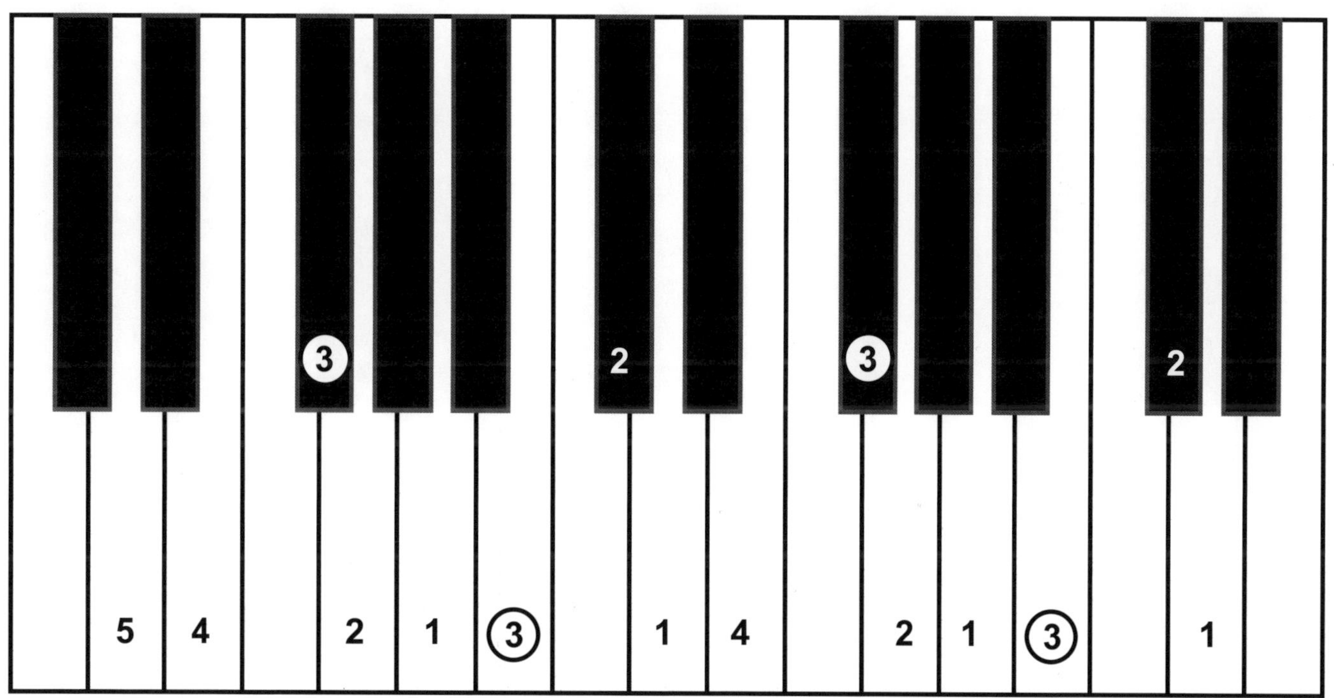

Group 1
D Major Scale
LH PLAY THE CHORD

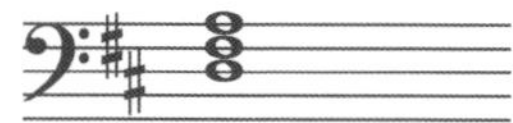

Group 1
A Major Scale
RH PLAY THE CHORD

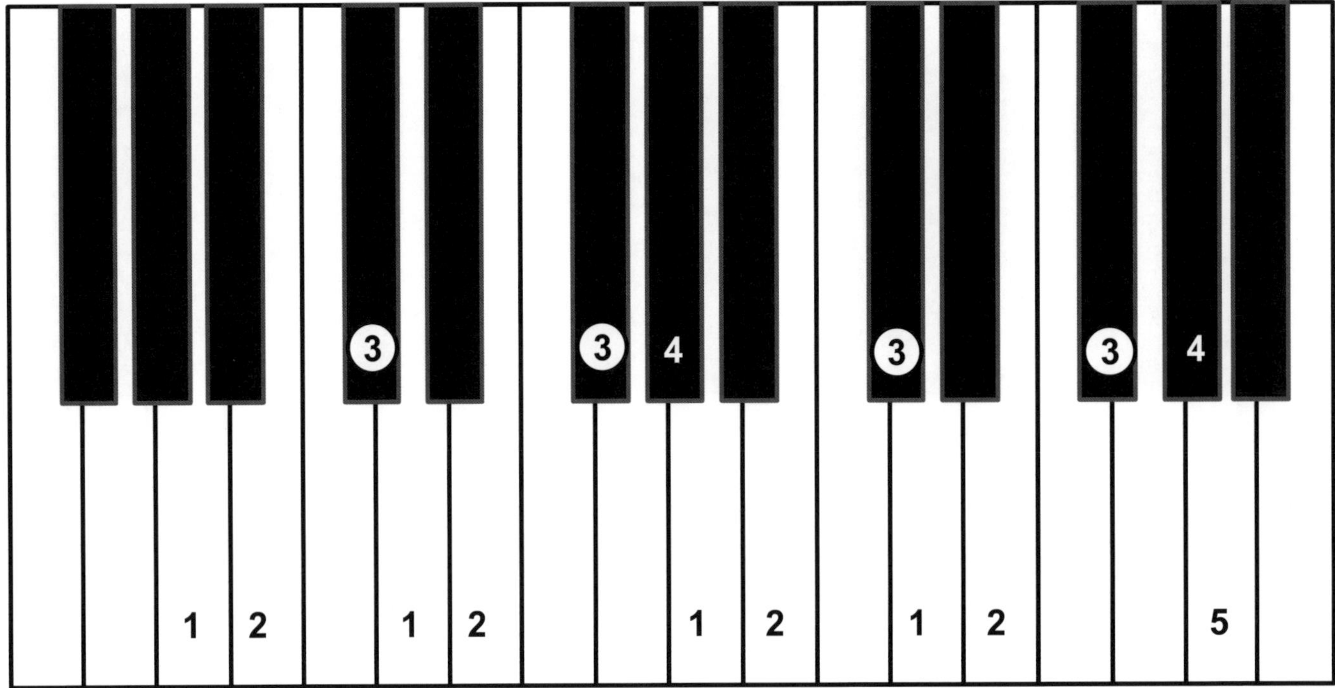

3rd fingers play together

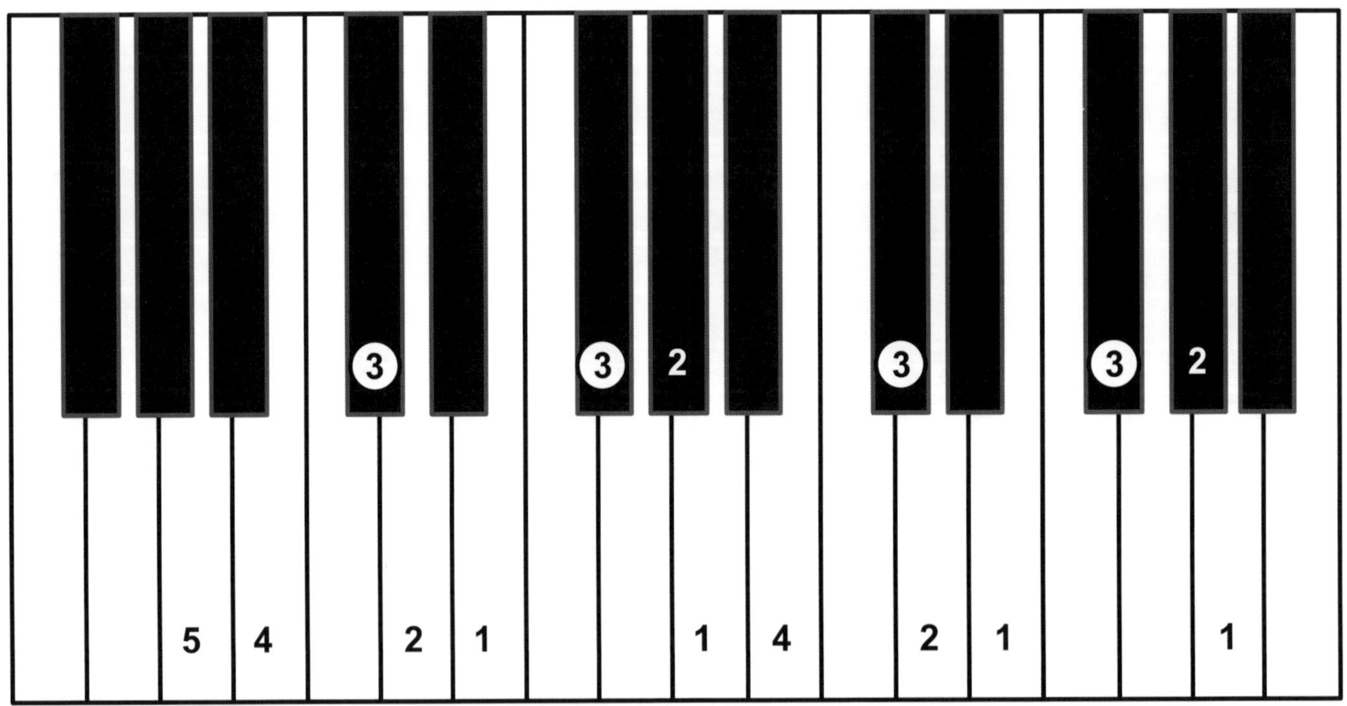

Group 1
A Major Scale
LH PLAY THE CHORD

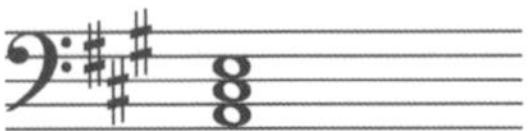

Group 1

E Major Scale

RH PLAY THE CHORD

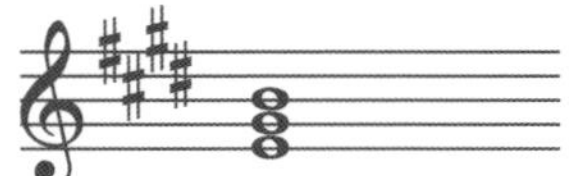

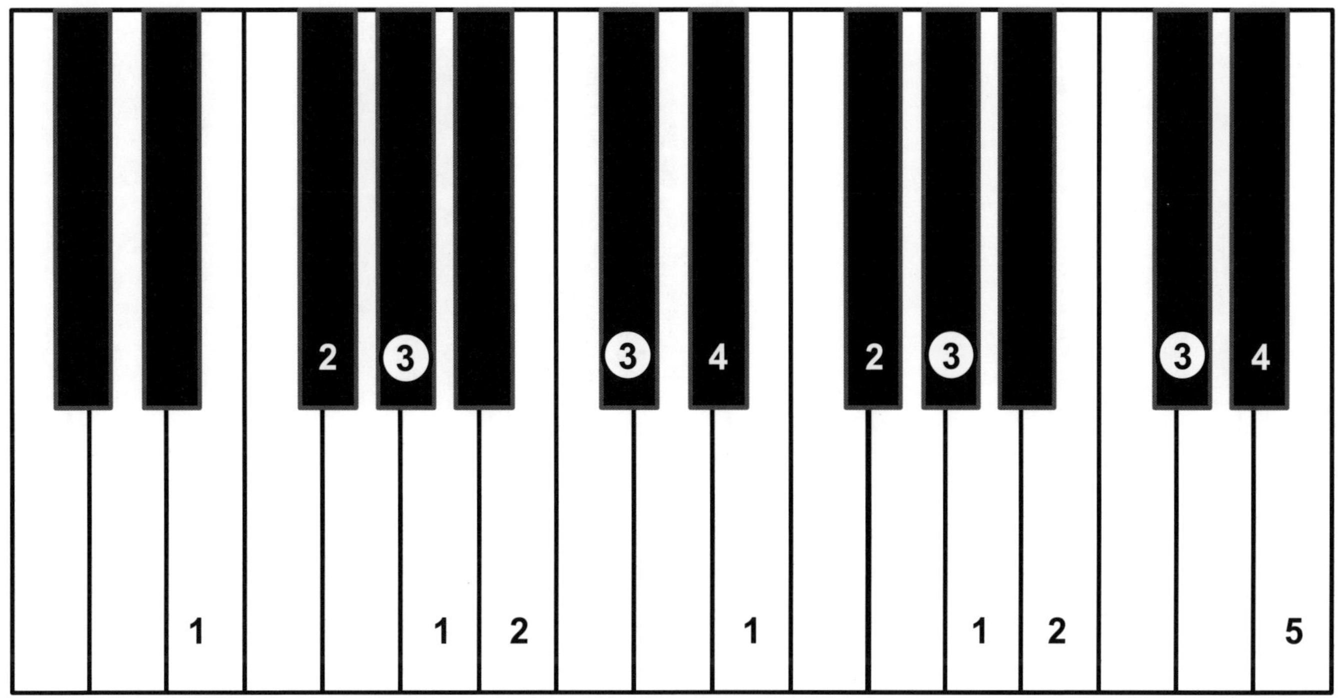

3rd fingers play together

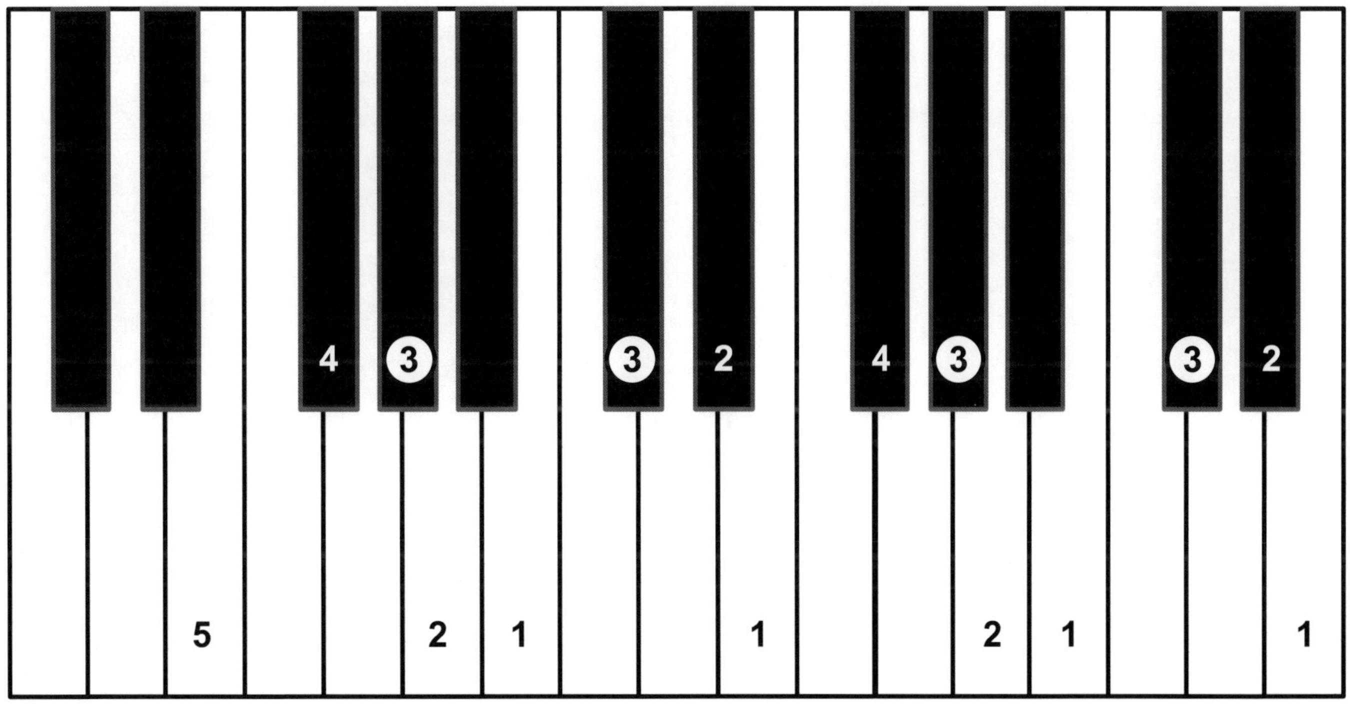

Group 1

E Major Scale

LH PLAY THE CHORD

Group 1

A Minor Scale

RH PLAY THE CHORD

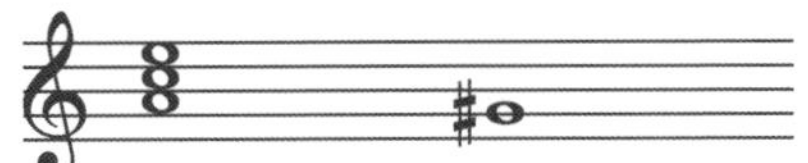

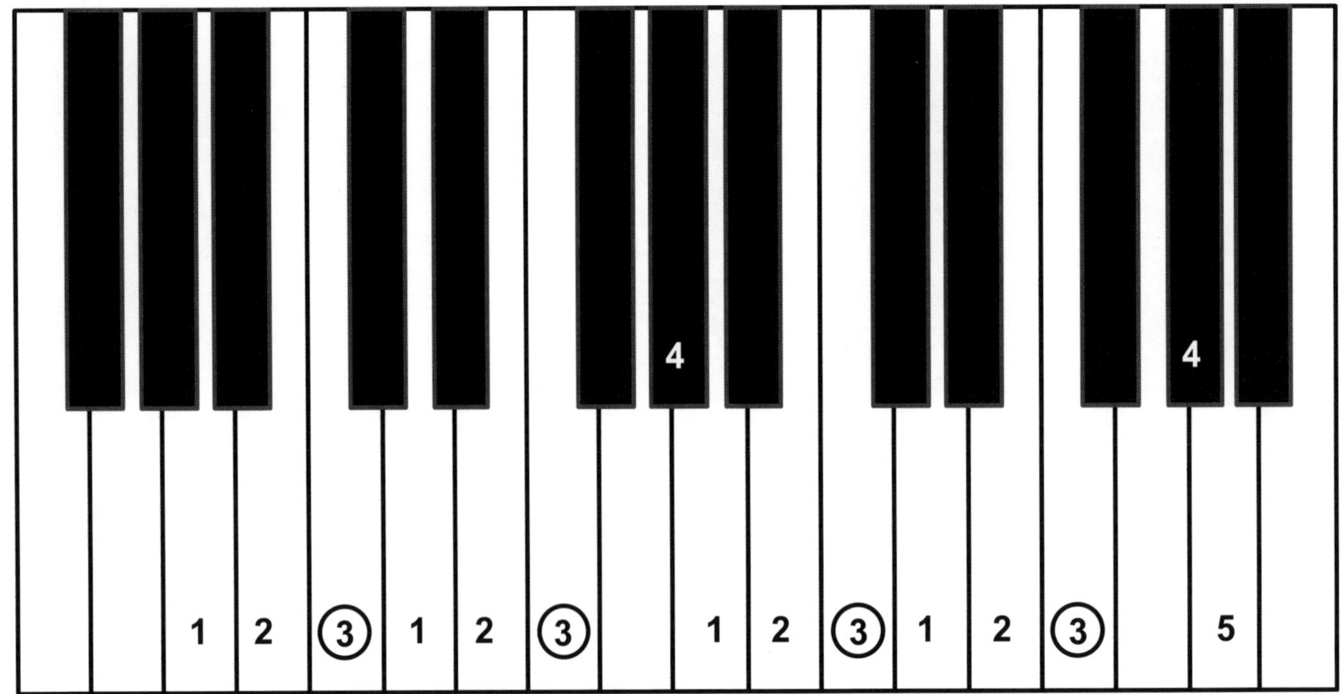

3rd fingers play together

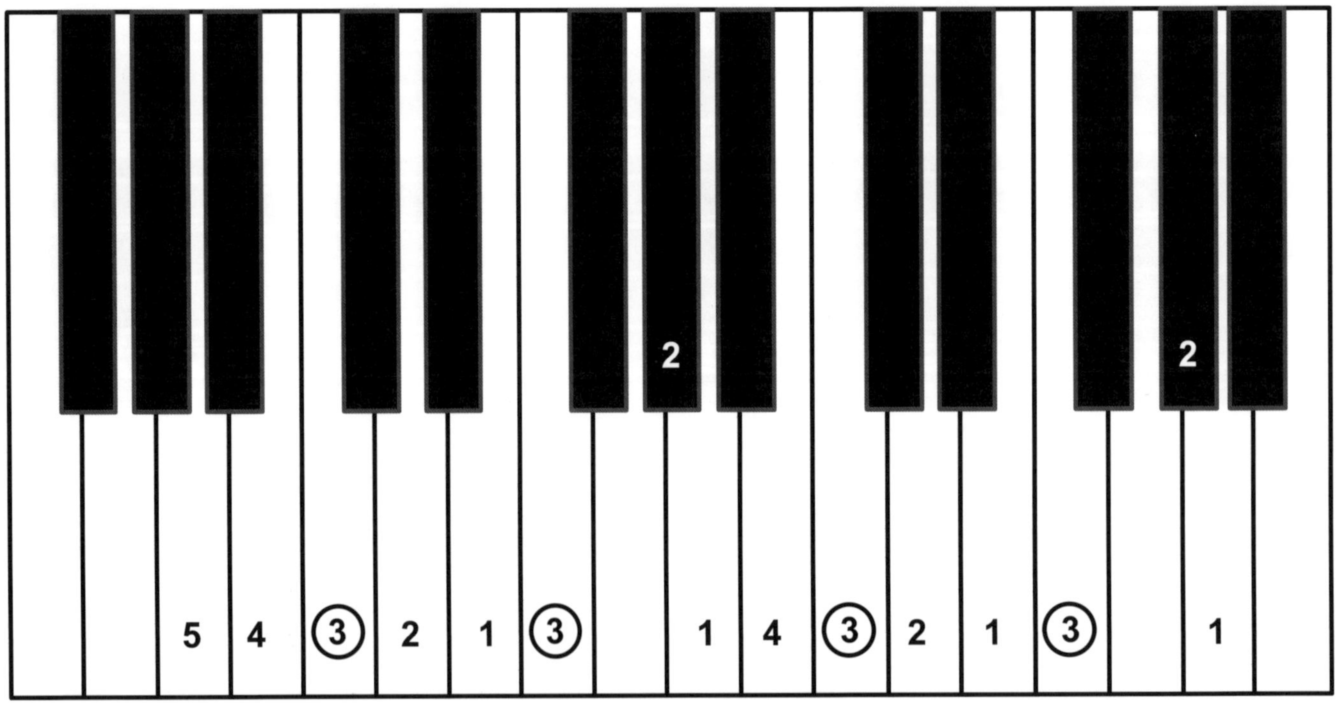

Group 1

A Minor Scale

LH PLAY THE CHORD

Group 1
D Minor Scale
RH PLAY THE CHORD

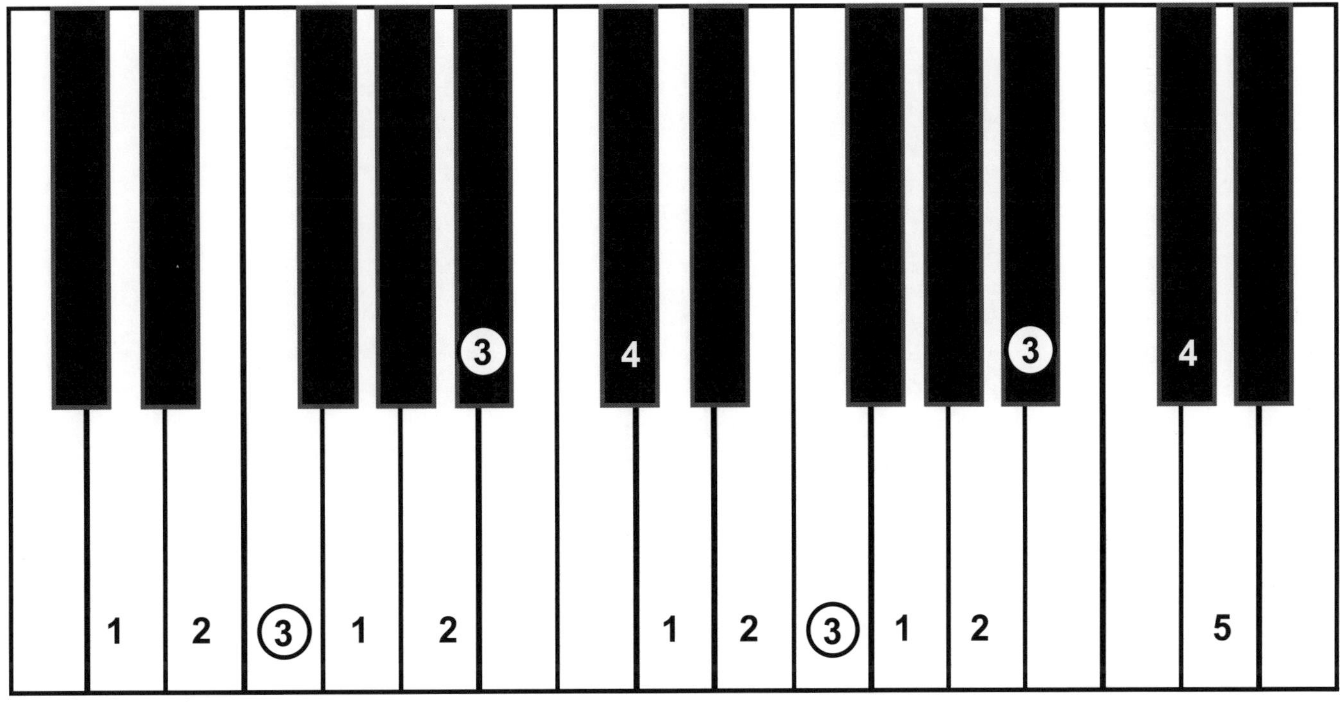

3rd fingers play together

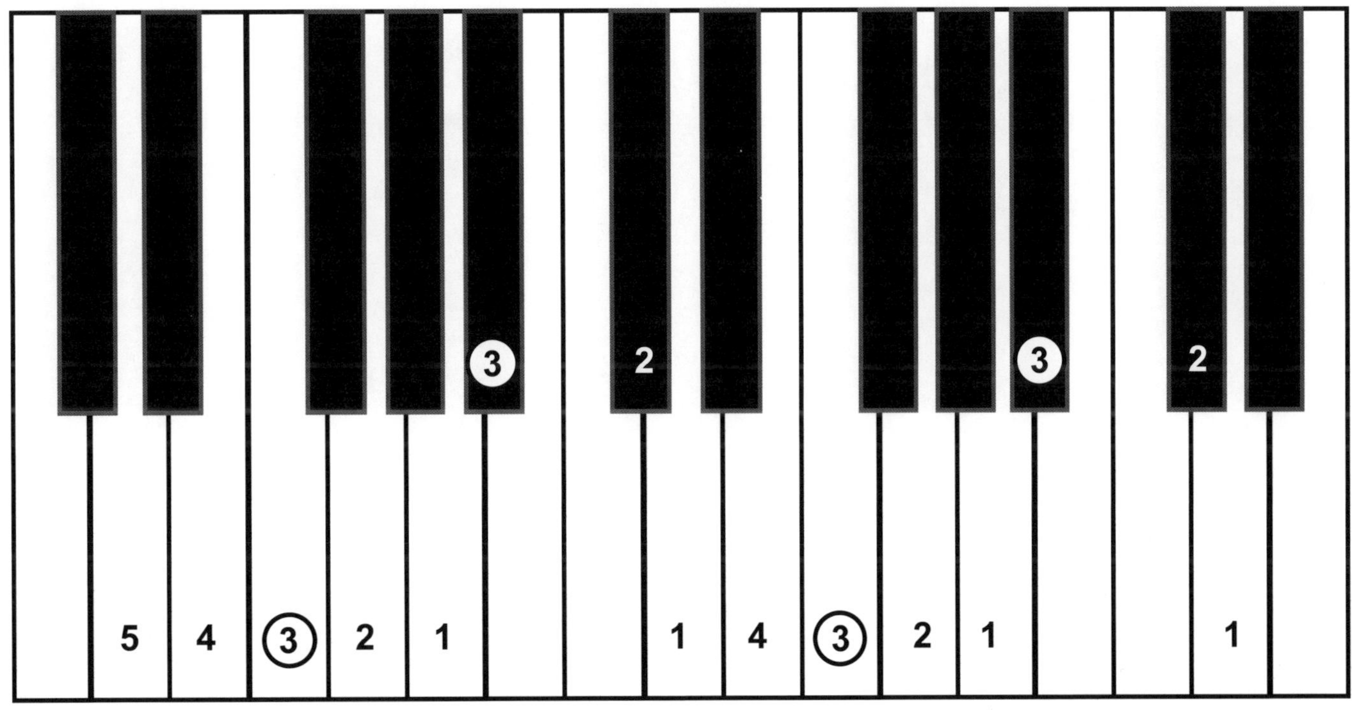

Group 1
D Minor Scale
LH PLAY THE CHORD

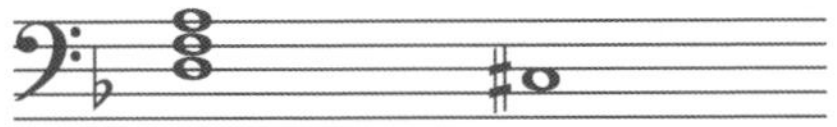

Group 1
E Minor Scale
RH PLAY THE CHORD

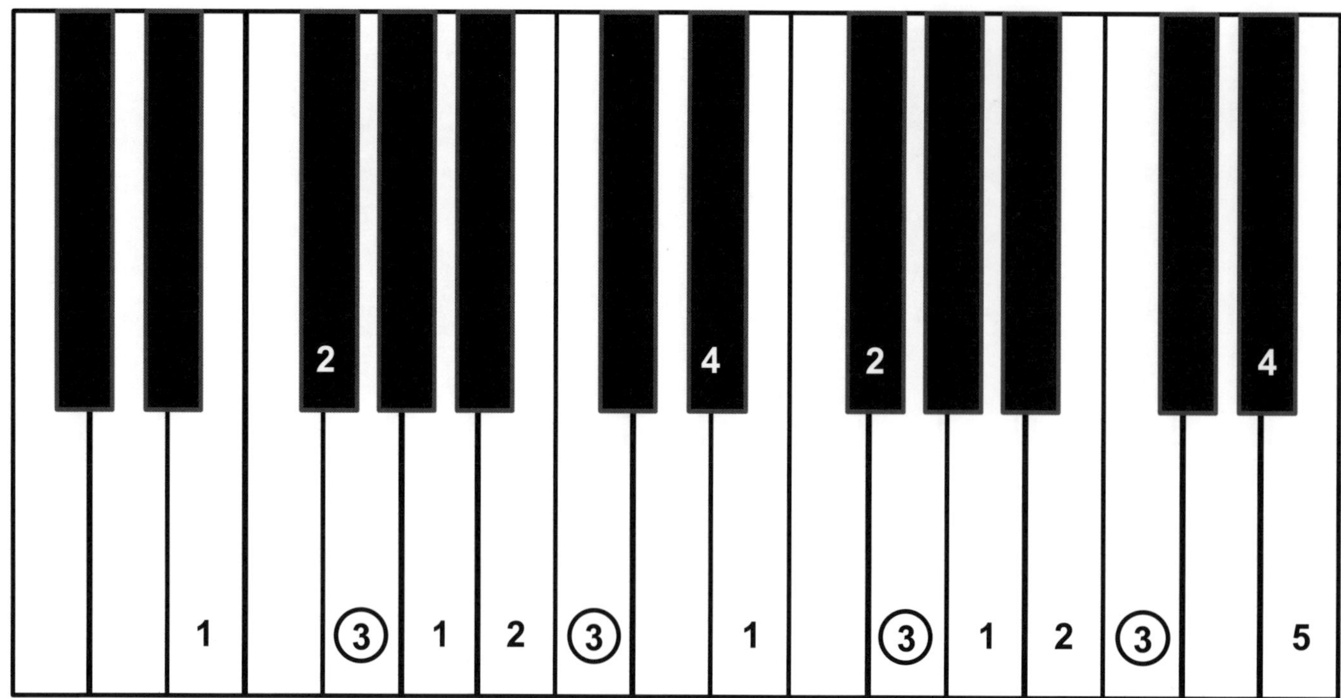

3rd fingers play together

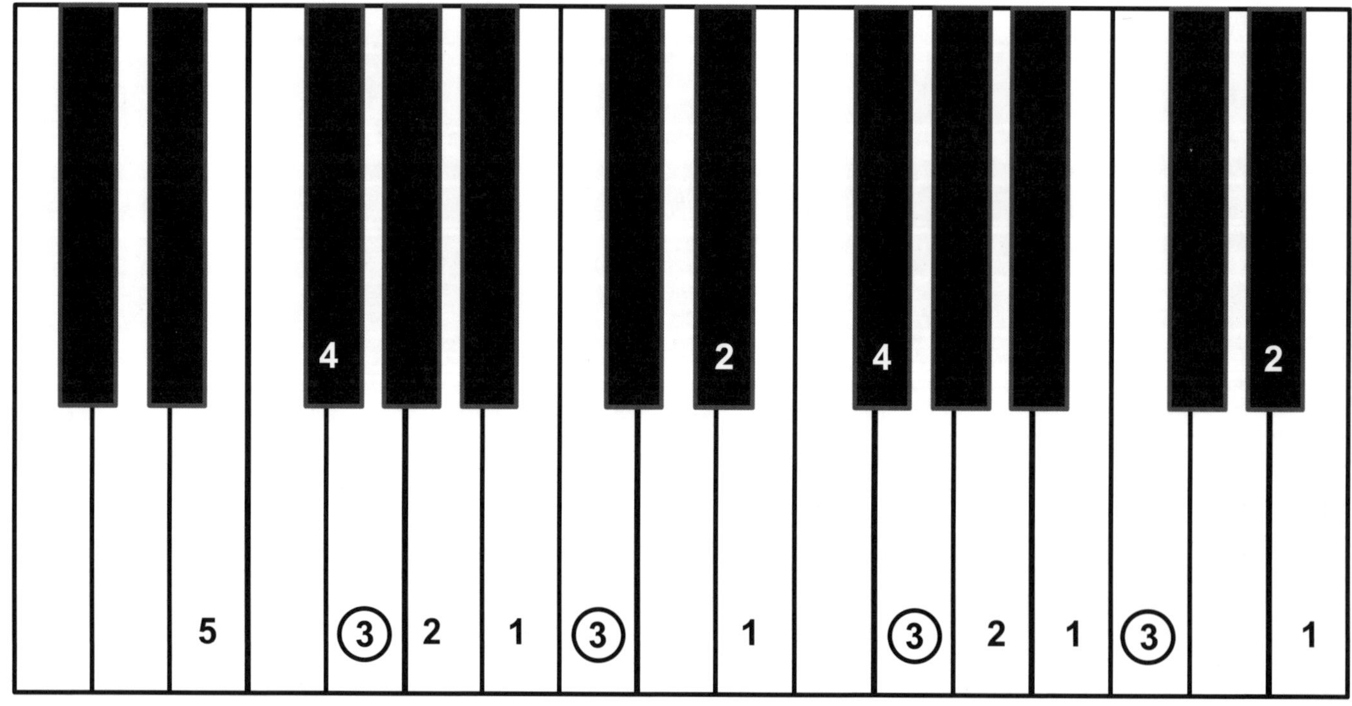

Group 1
E Minor Scale
LH PLAY THE CHORD

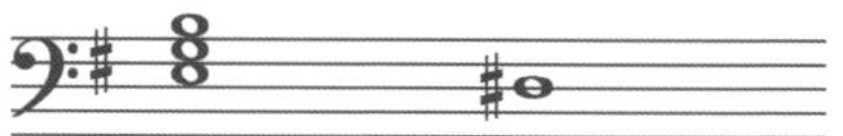

Group 1
C Minor Scale
RH PLAY THE CHORD

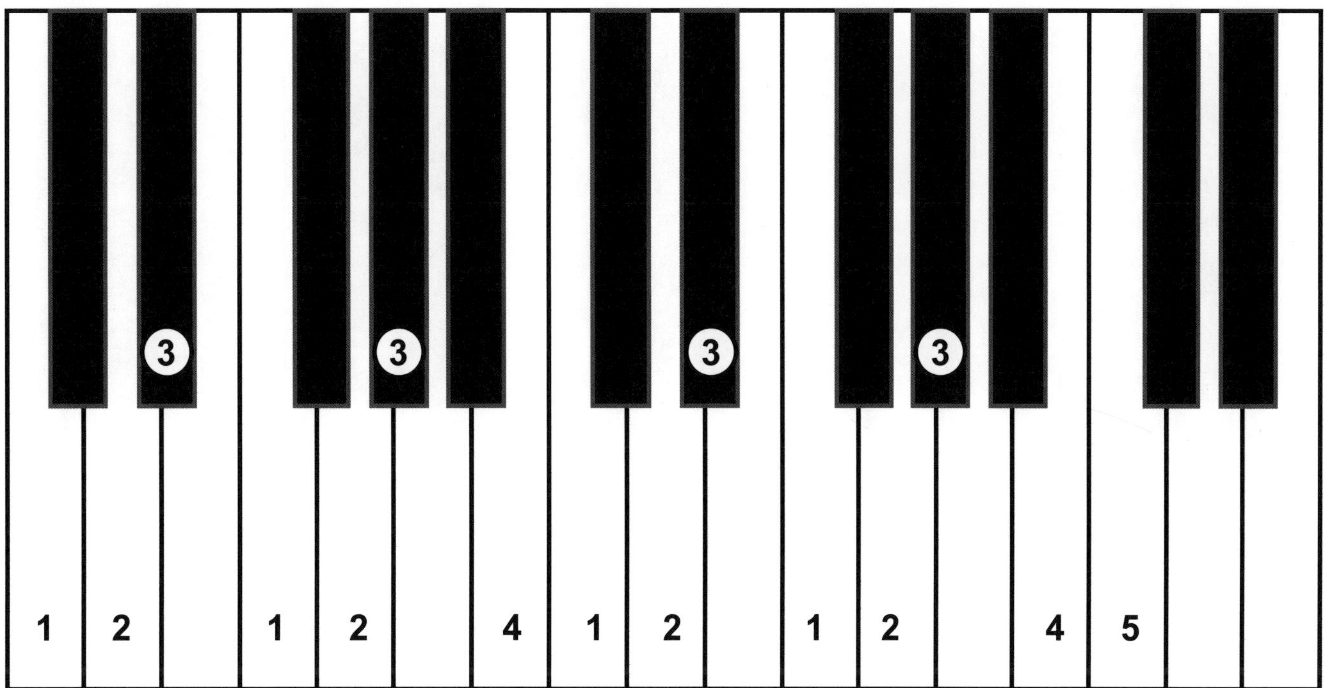

3rd fingers play together

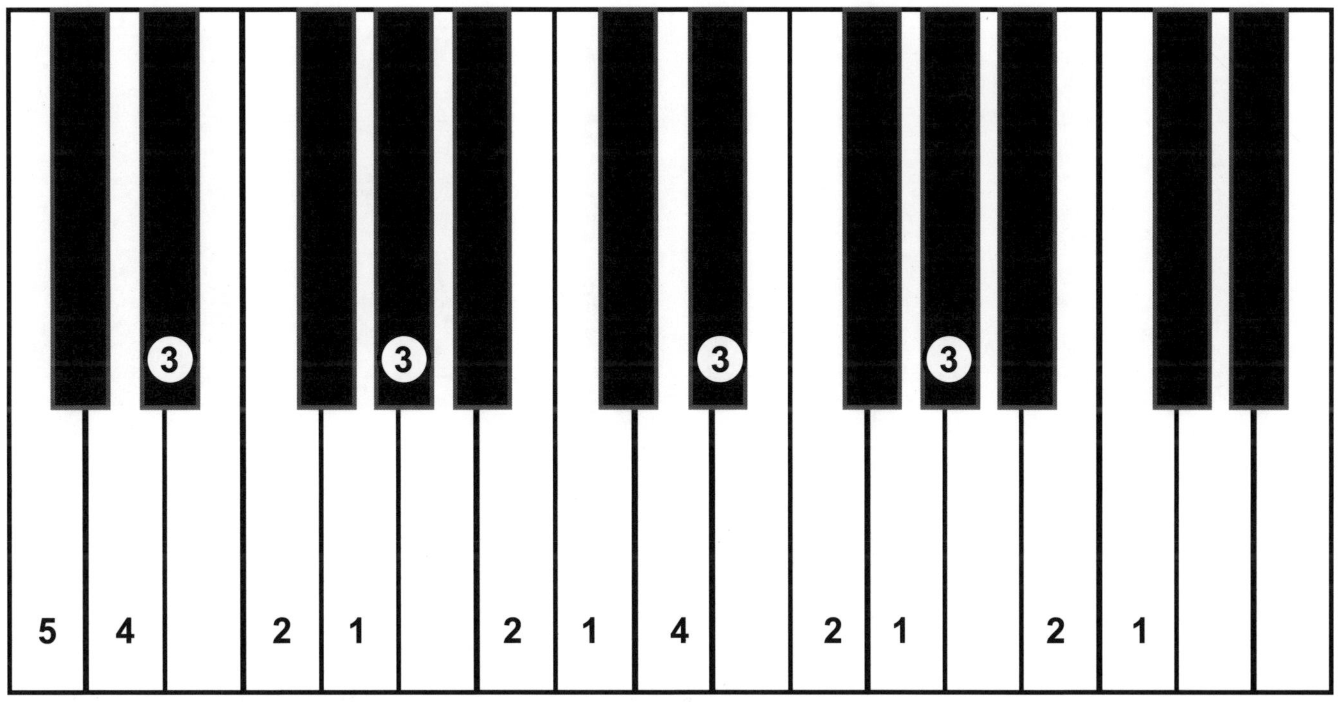

Group 1
C Minor Scale
LH PLAY THE CHORD

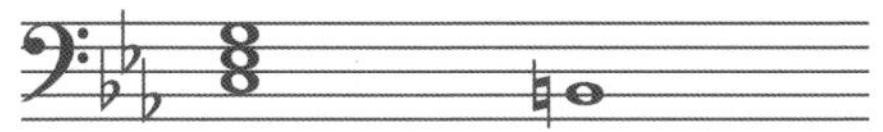

Group 1

G Minor Scale

RH PLAY THE CHORD

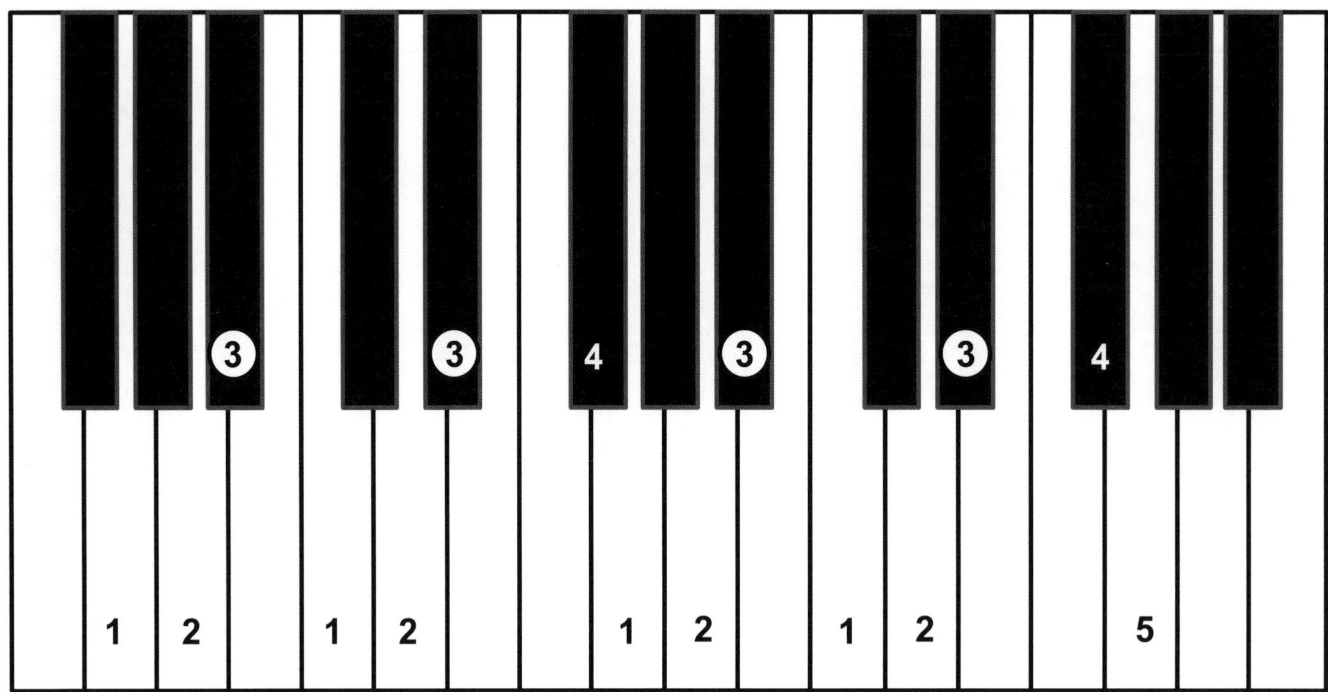

3rd fingers play together

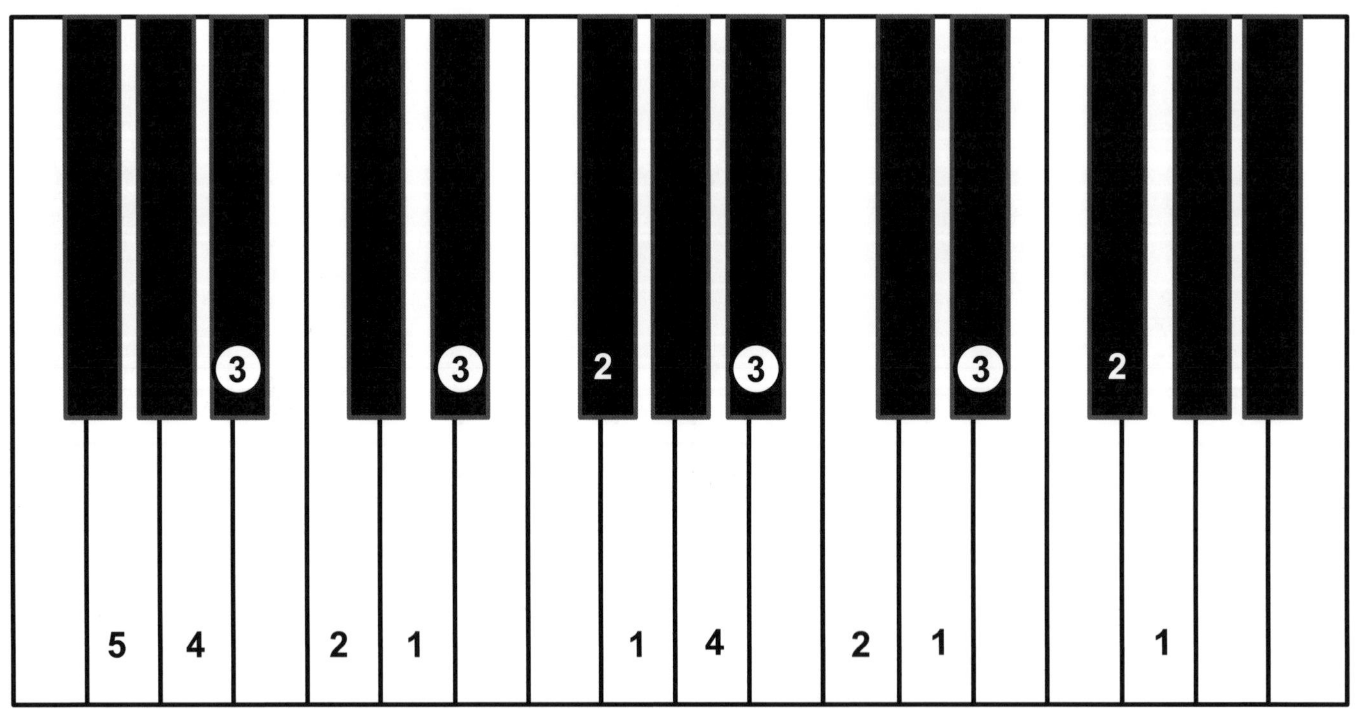

Group 1

G Minor Scale

LH PLAY THE CHORD

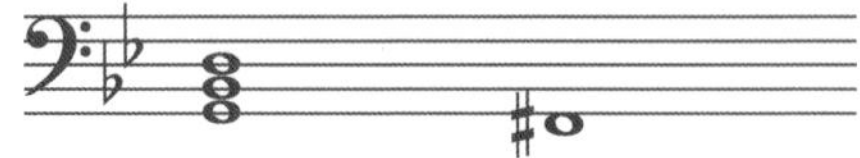

Group 1
Ab major Scale
RH PLAY THE CHORD

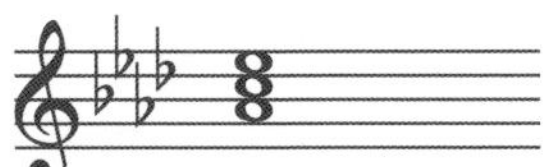

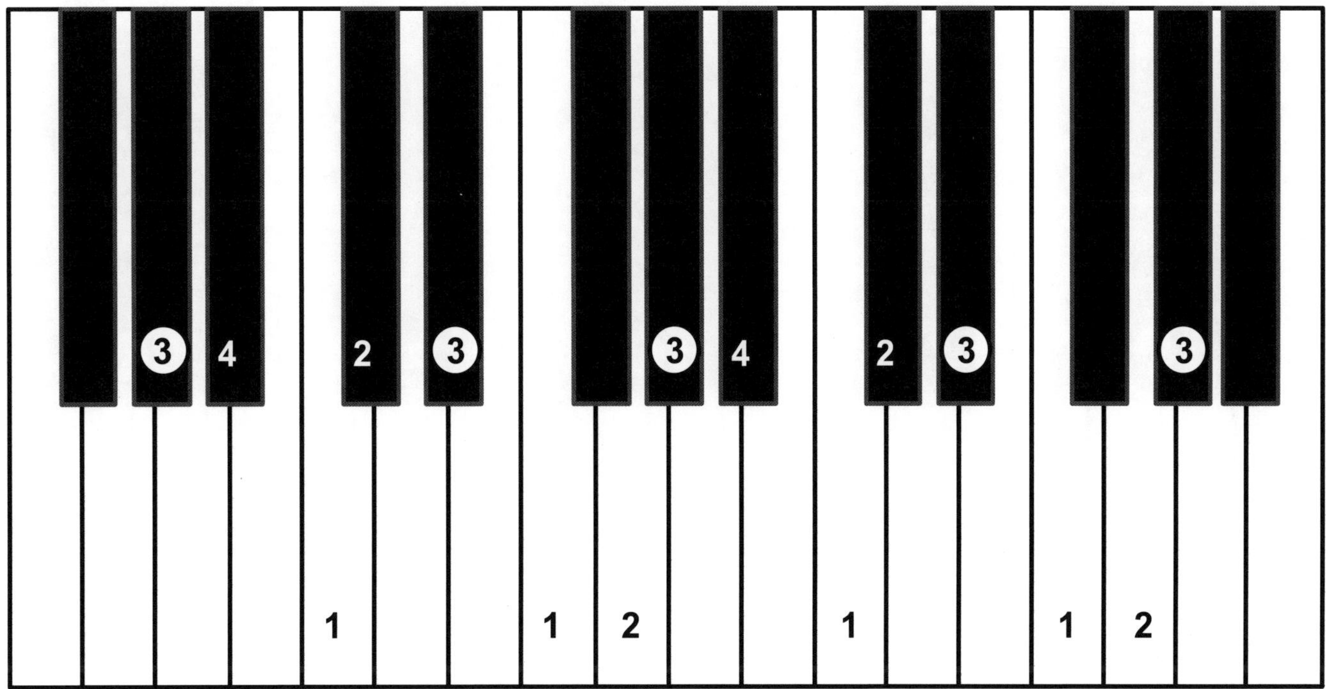

3rd fingers play together

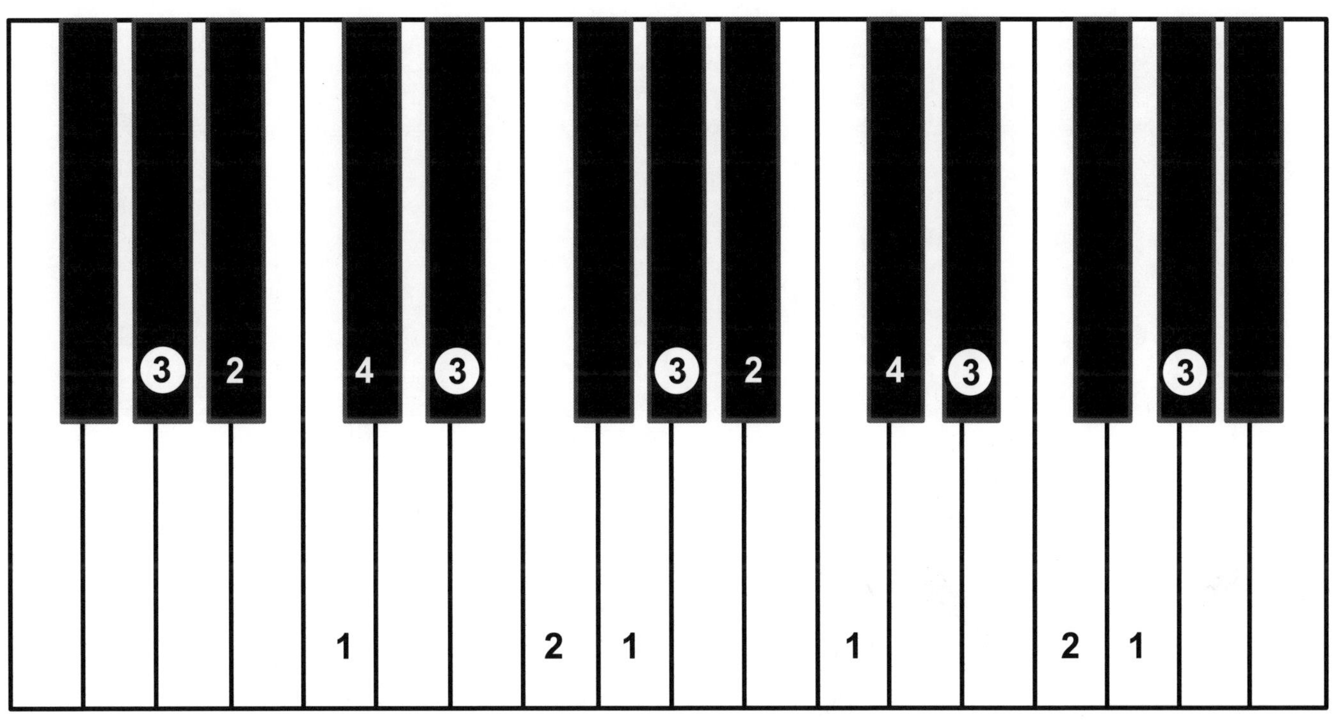

Group 1
Ab major Scale
LH PLAY THE CHORD

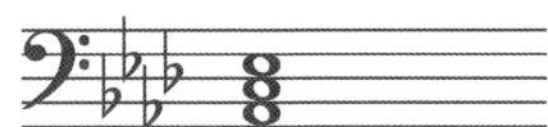

Group 1
G# Minor Scale
RH PLAY THE CHORD

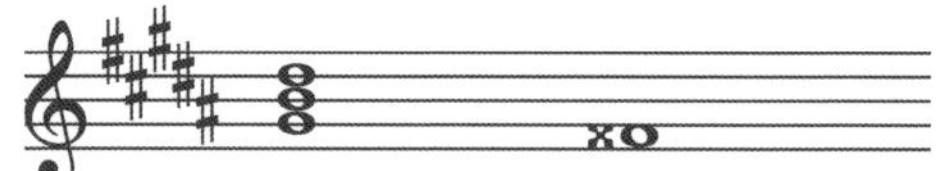

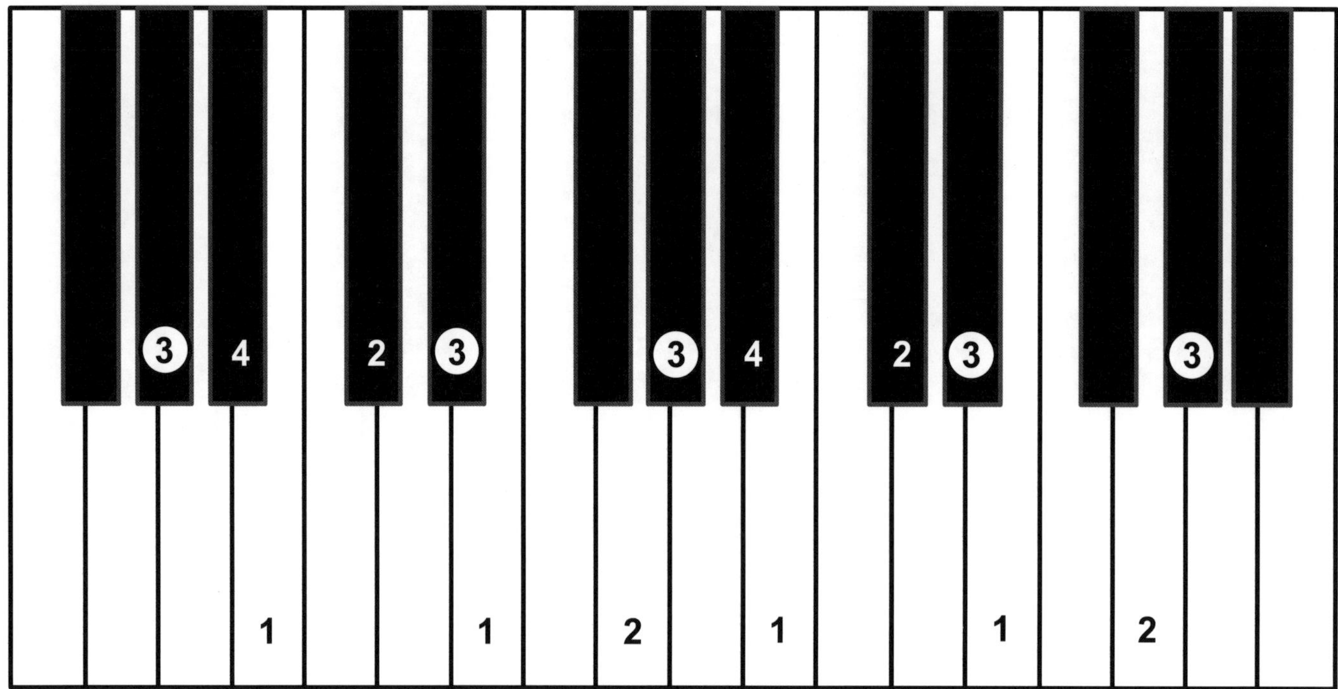

3rd fingers play together

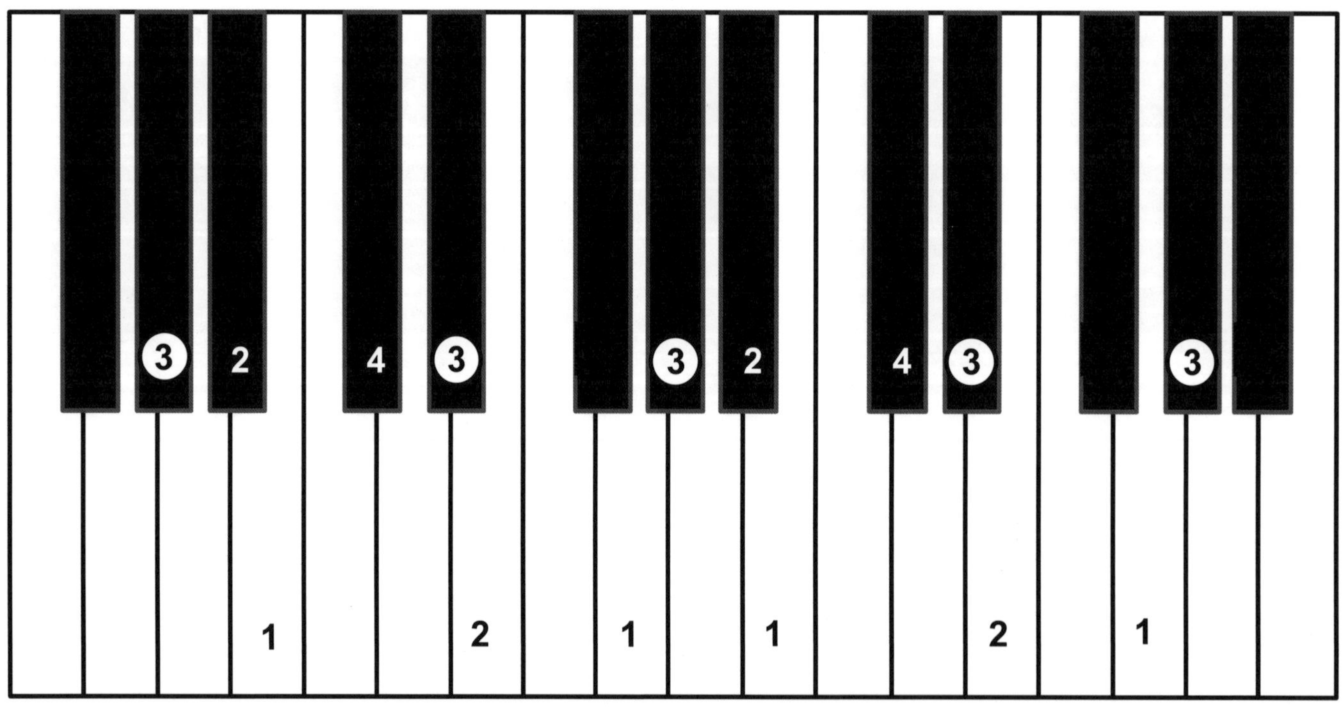

Group 1
G# Minor Scale
LH PLAY THE CHORD

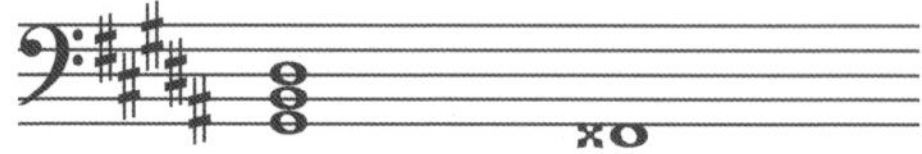

Group 1
C# Minor Scale
RH PLAY THE CHORD

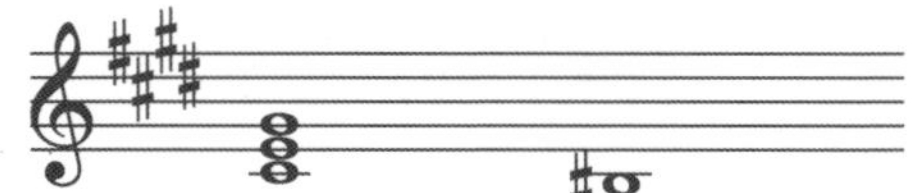

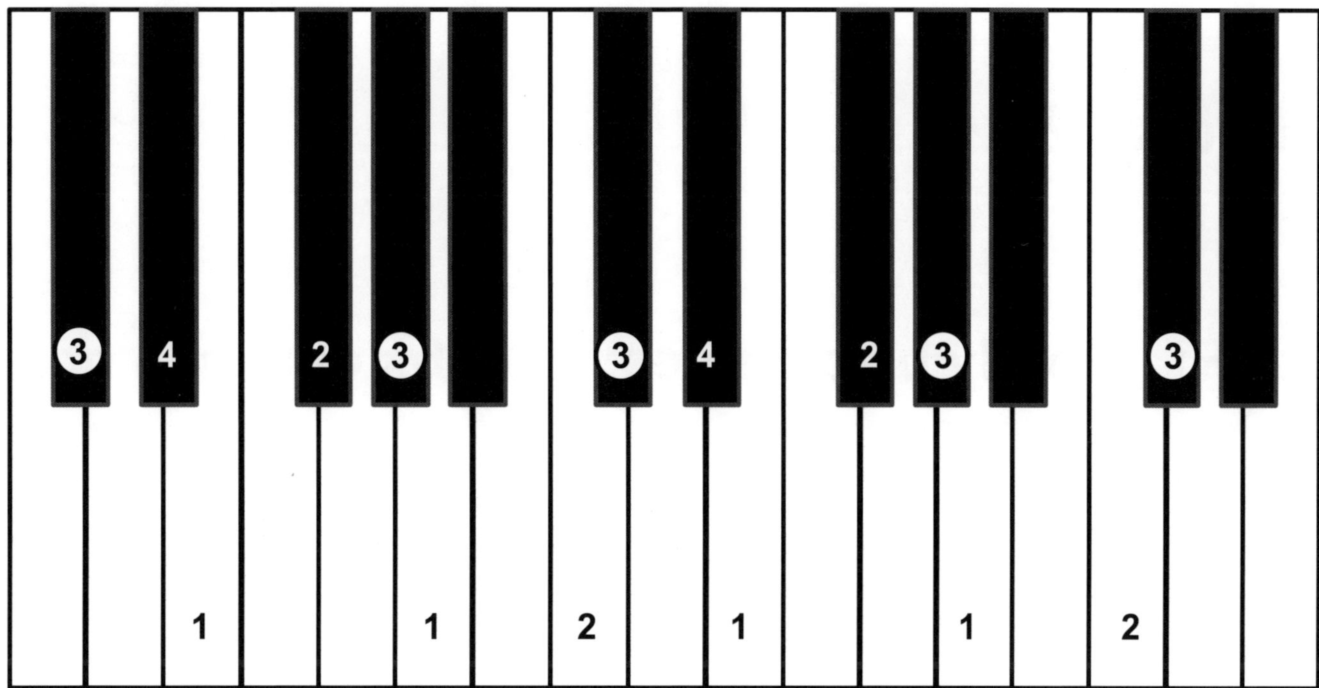

3rd fingers play together

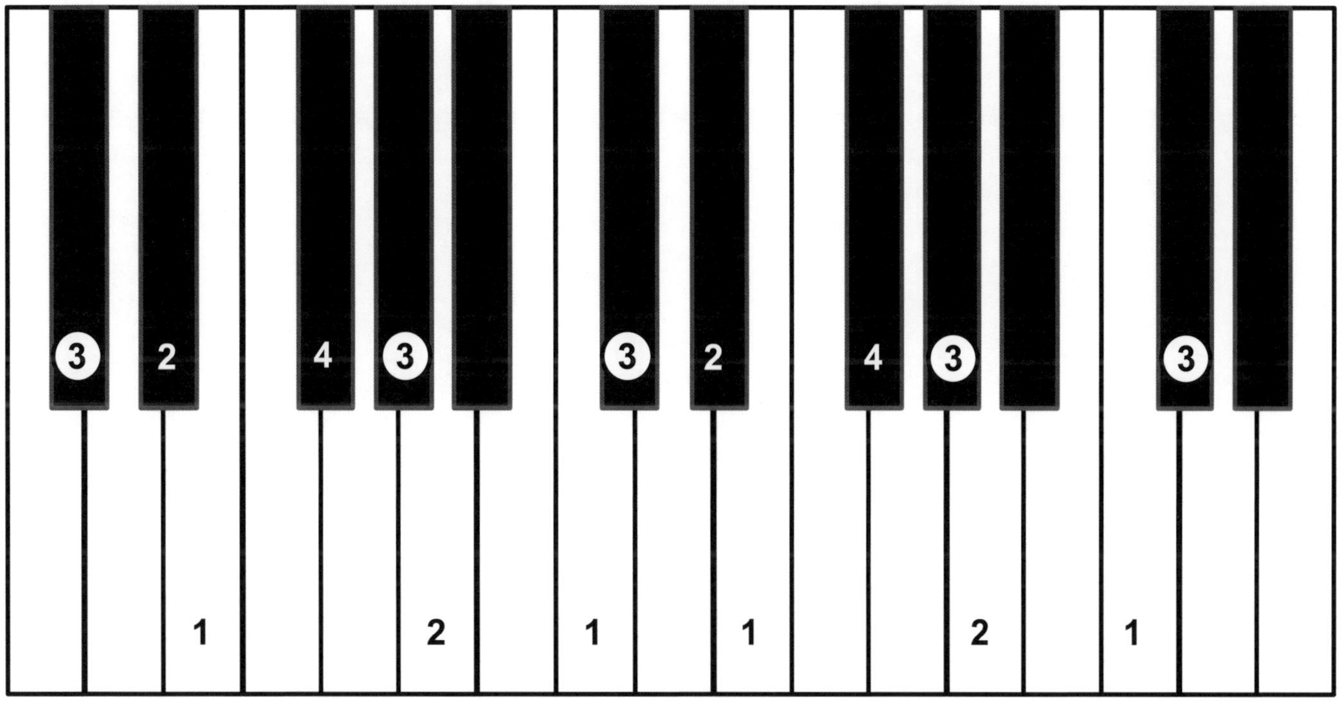

Group 1
C# Minor Scale
LH PLAY THE CHORD

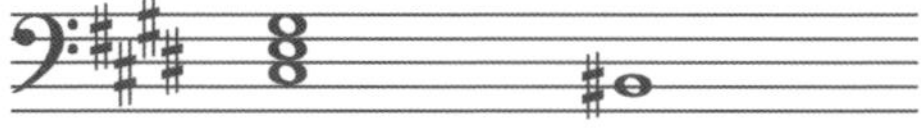

Scales

Group 2

RULE: Mostly black notes, thumbs on white notes

B major	F# major	Db major

Tip:

- Check the semitones between 3/4 and 7/8 for the correct white notes.

Group 2
B Major Scale
RH PLAY THE CHORD

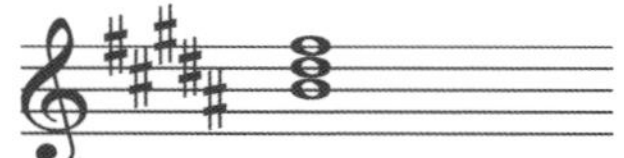

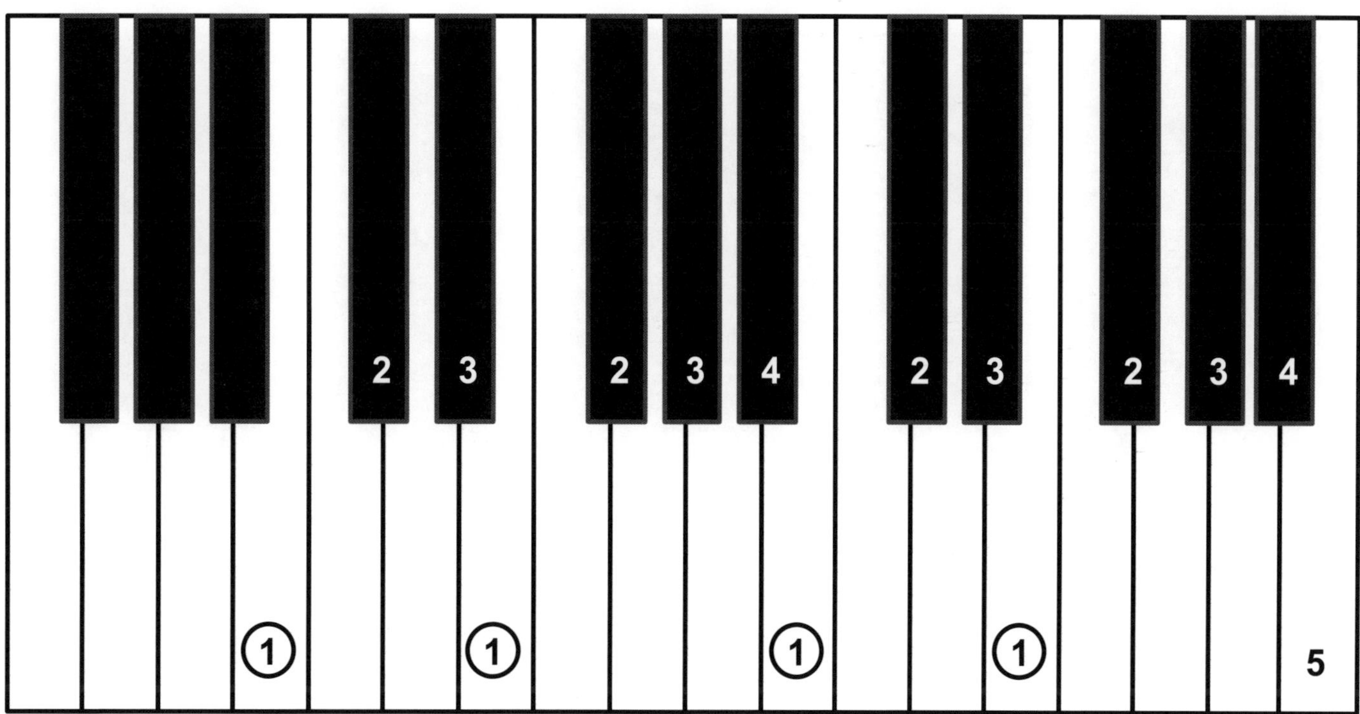

Thumbs on white notes

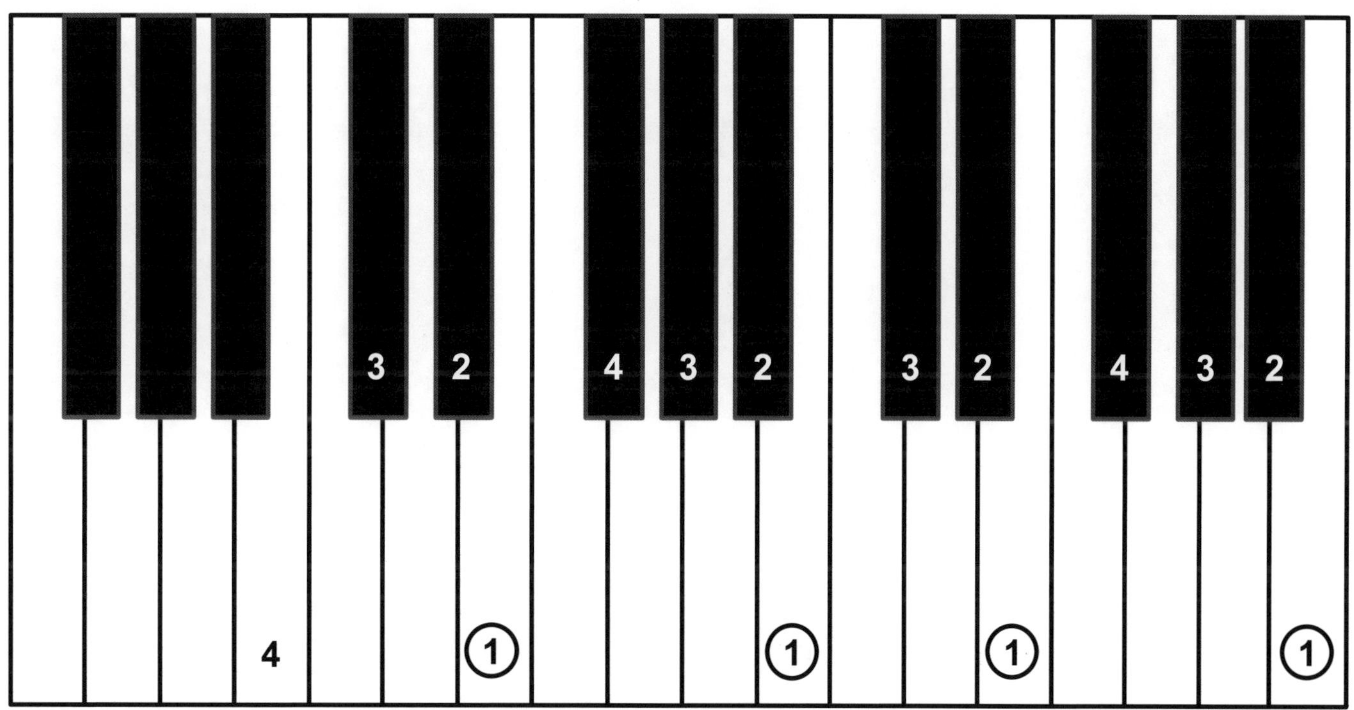

Group 1
B Major Scale
LH PLAY THE CHORD

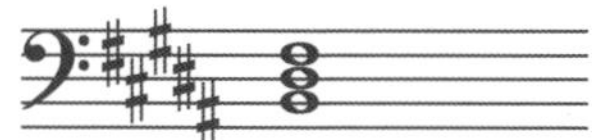

Group 2
F# Major Scale
RH PLAY THE CHORD

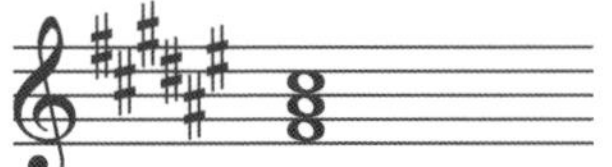

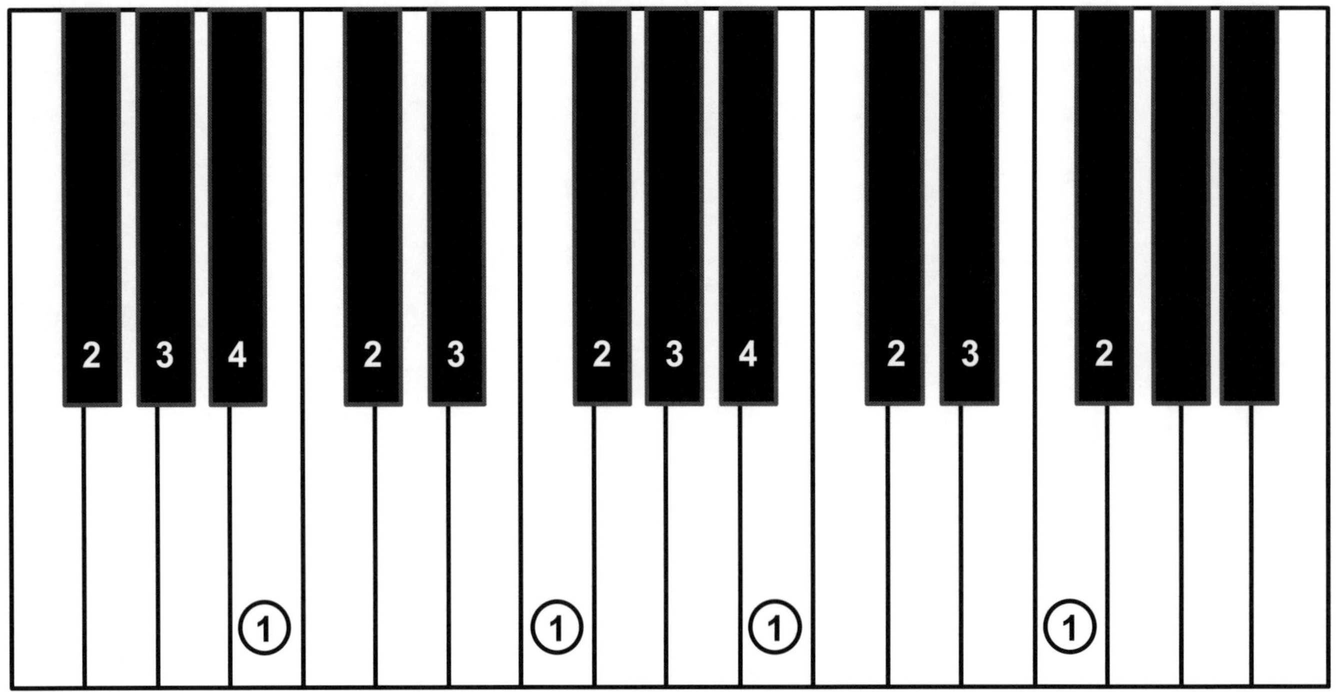

Thumbs on white notes

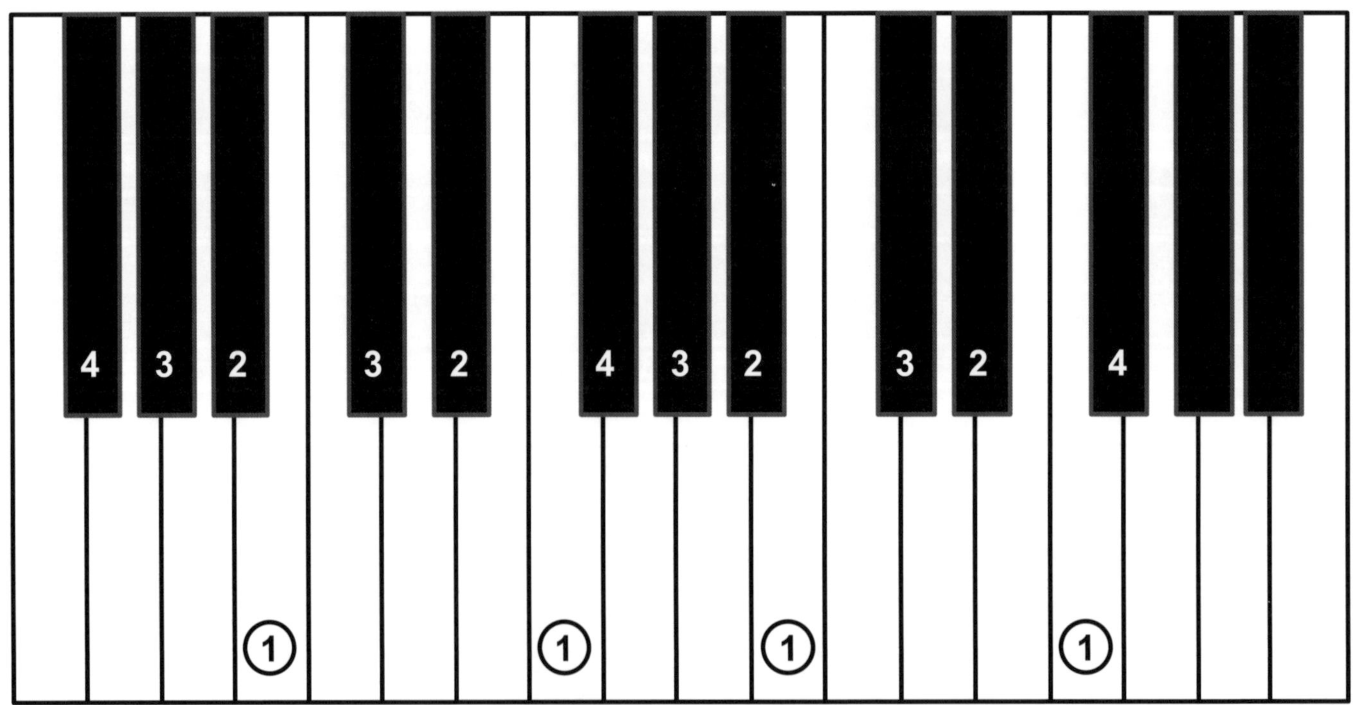

Group 2
F# Major Scale
LH PLAY THE CHORD

Group 2
Db Major Scale
RH PLAY THE CHORD

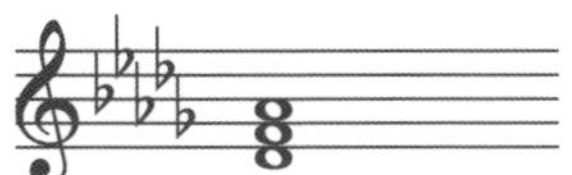

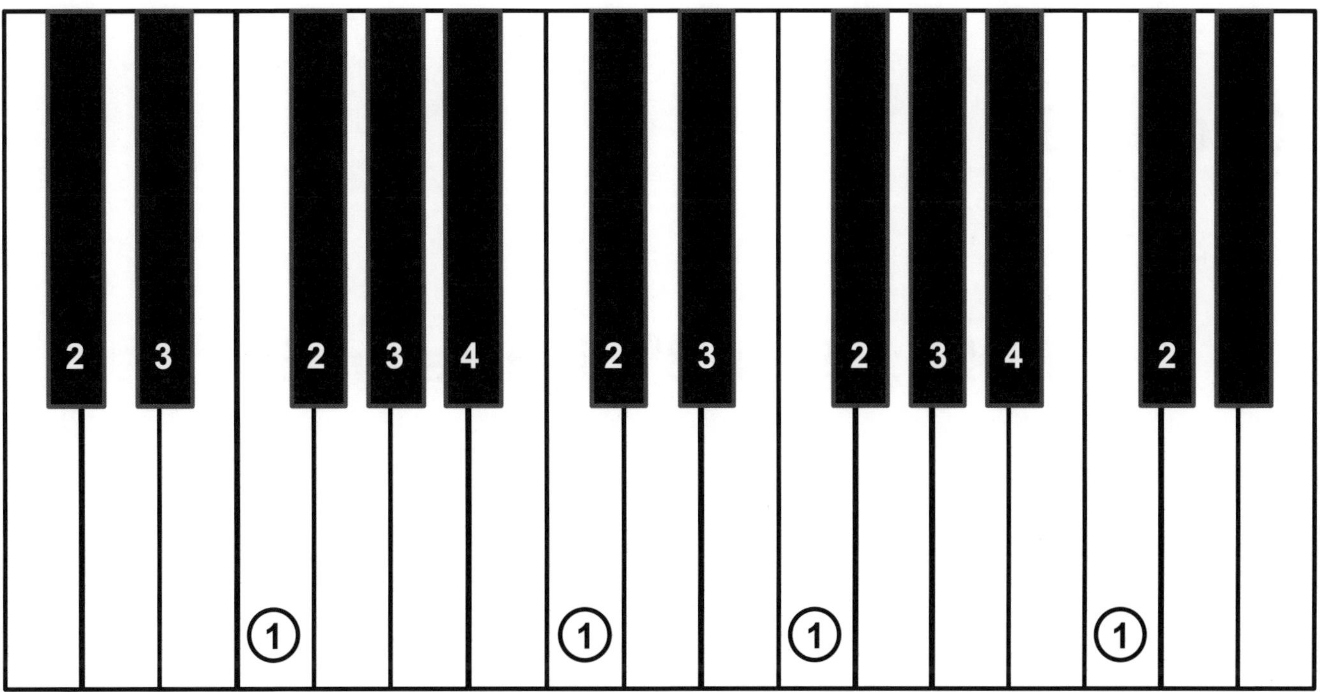

Thumbs on white notes

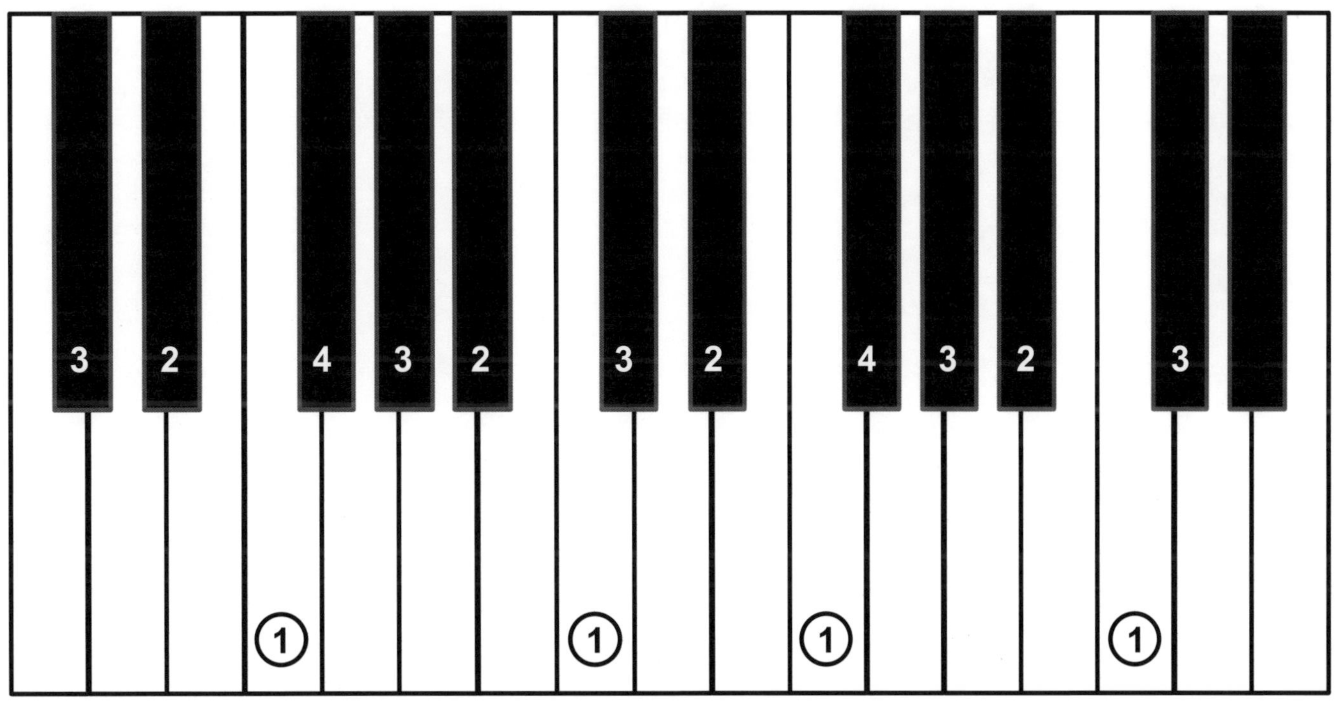

Group 2
Db Major Scale
LH PLAY THE CHORD

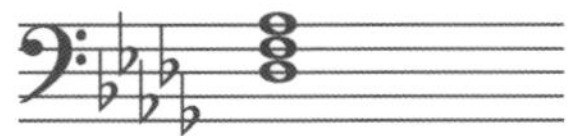

Scales

Group 3

RULE: Both 3rd fingers on Eb

Eb major

RULE: Opposite 3rd and 4th fingers on Bb and Eb

Bb major

Group 3
Eb Major Scale
RH PLAY THE CHORD

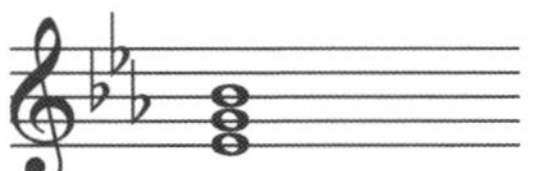

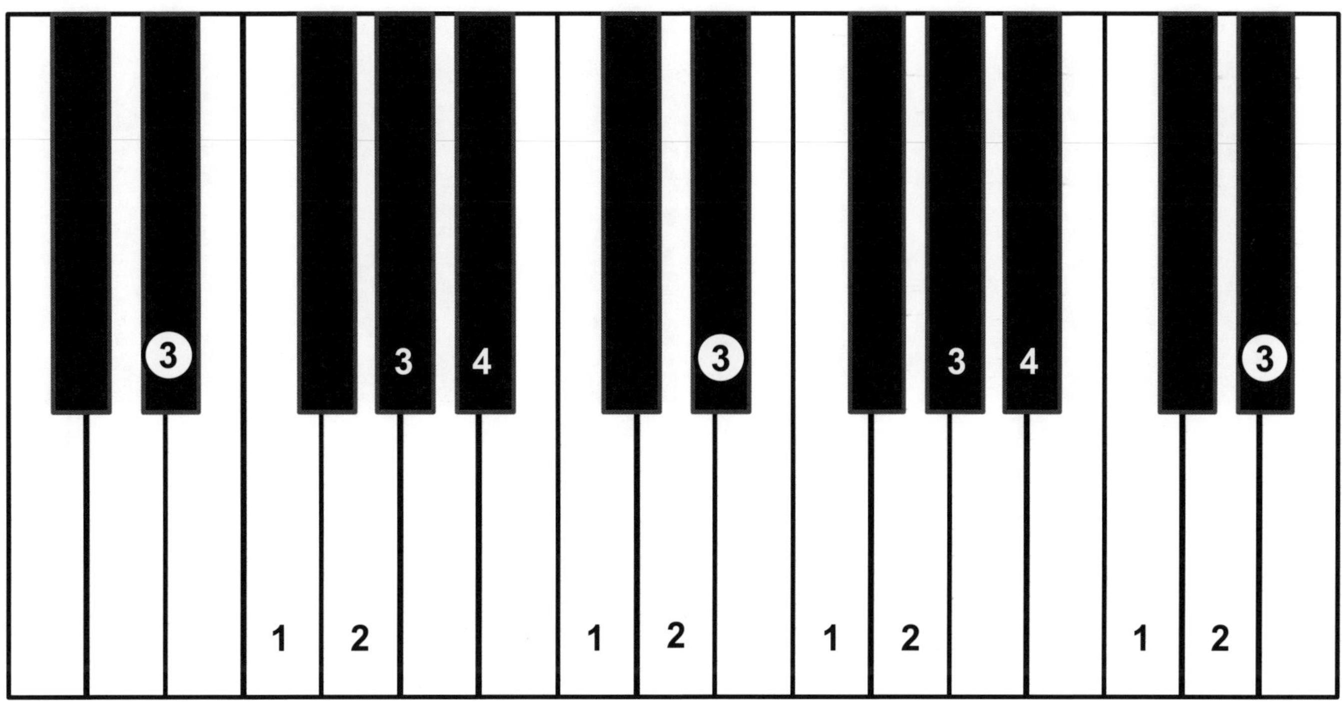

Both 3rd fingers on Eb

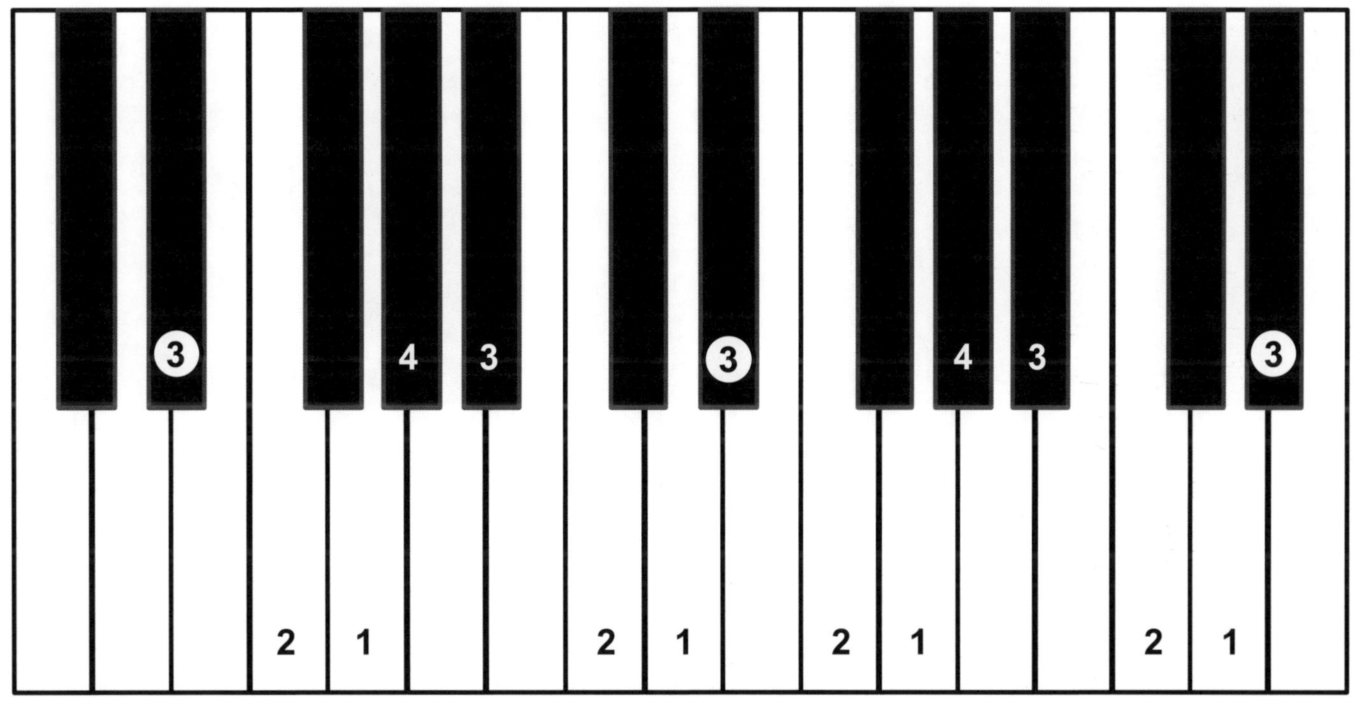

Group 3
Eb Major Scale
LH PLAY THE CHORD

Group 3
Bb Major Scale
RH PLAY THE CHORD

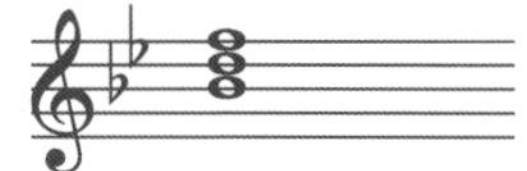

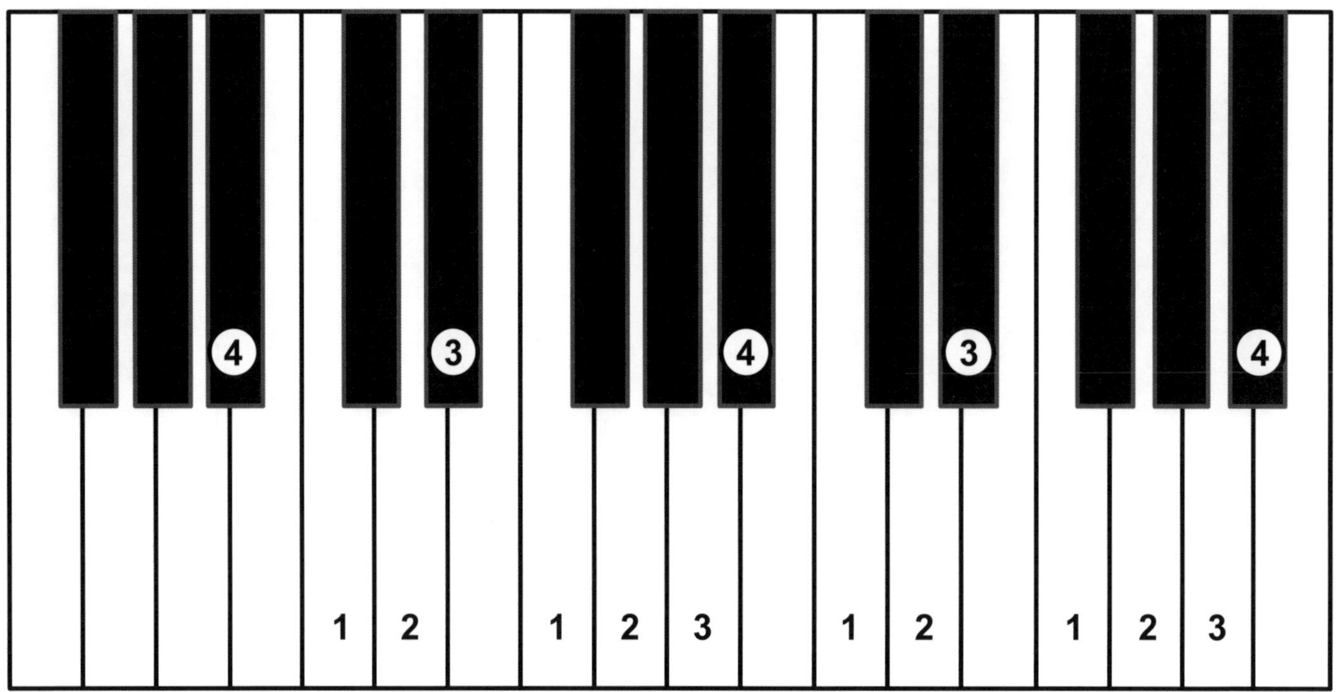

Opposite 3rd and 4th fingers on Eb and Bb

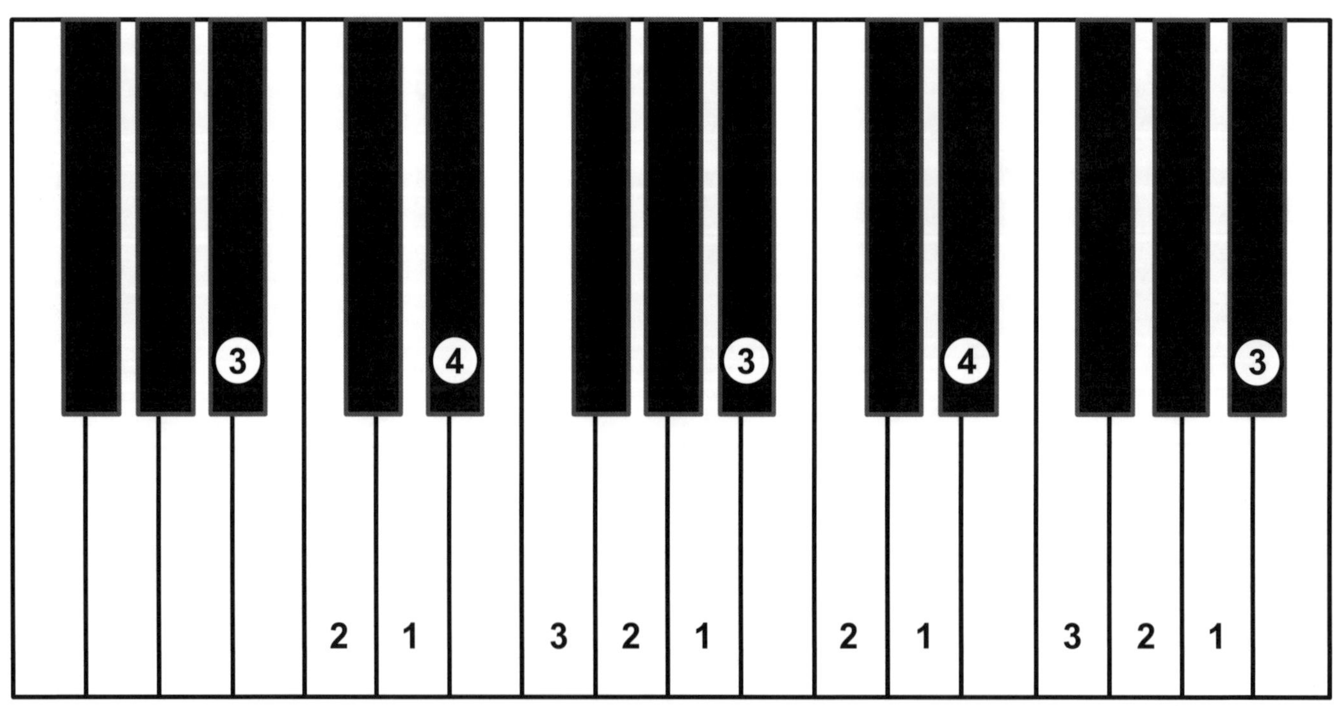

Group 3
Bb Major Scale
LH PLAY THE CHORD

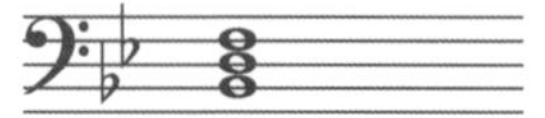

Scales

Group 4

RULE: Thumbs on C and F

F major F minor

Group 4

F Major Scale

RH PLAY THE CHORD

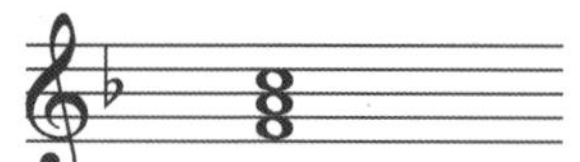

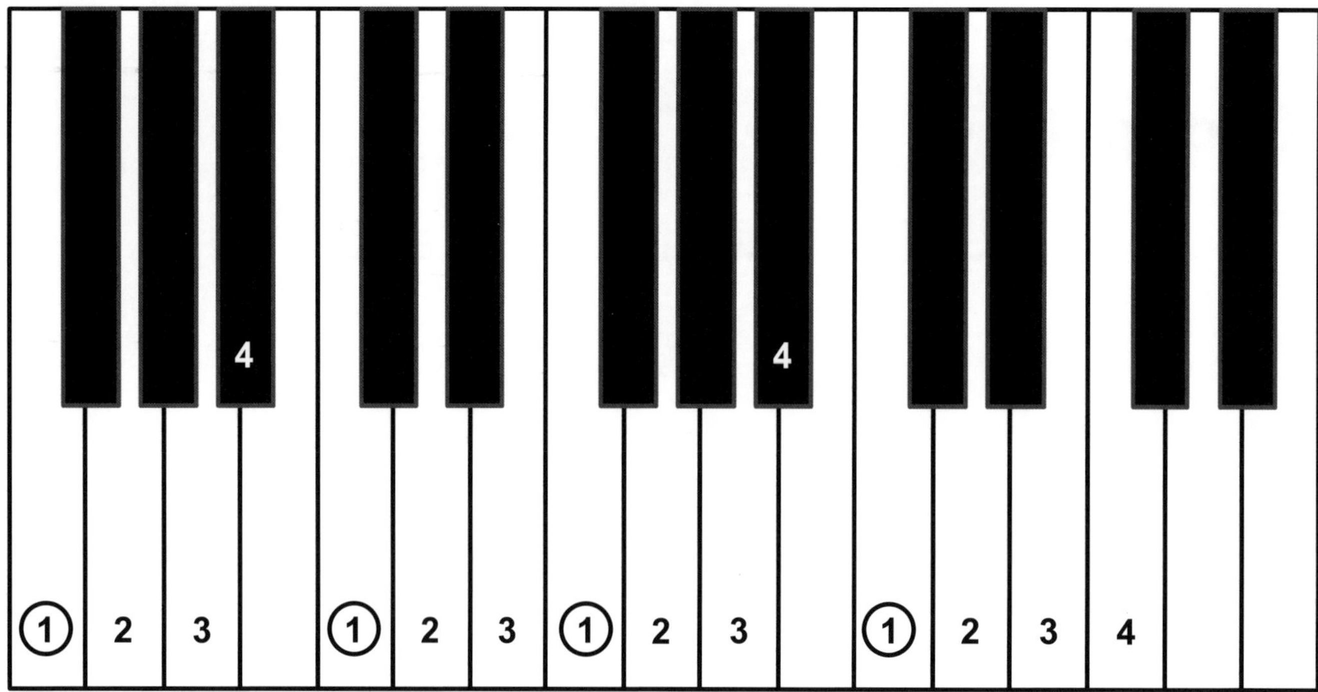

Thumbs on C and F

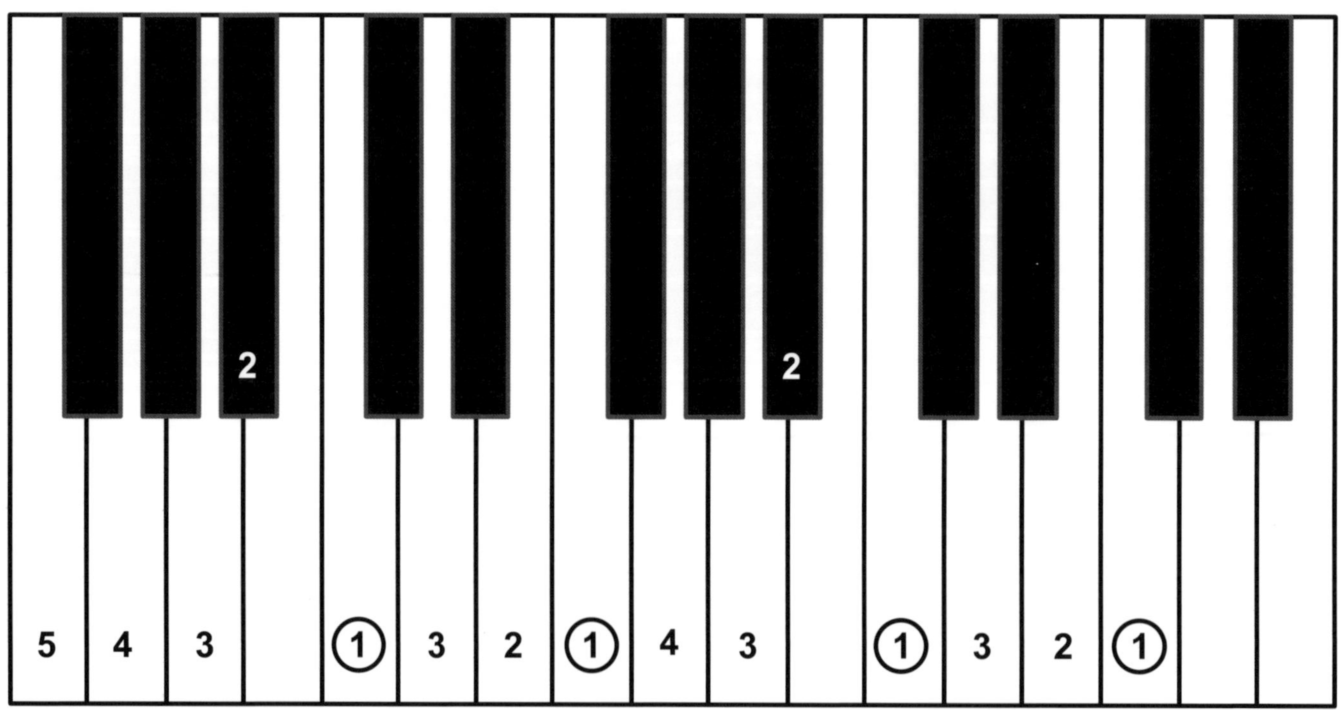

Group 4

F Major Scale

LH PLAY THE CHORD

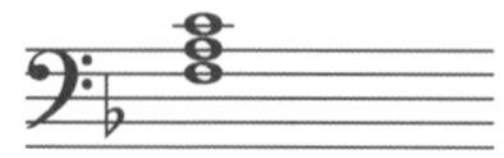

Group 4
F Minor Scale
RH PLAY THE CHORD

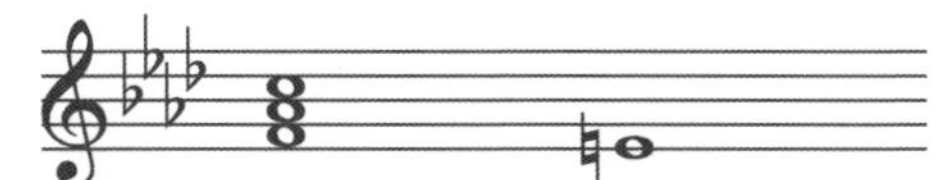

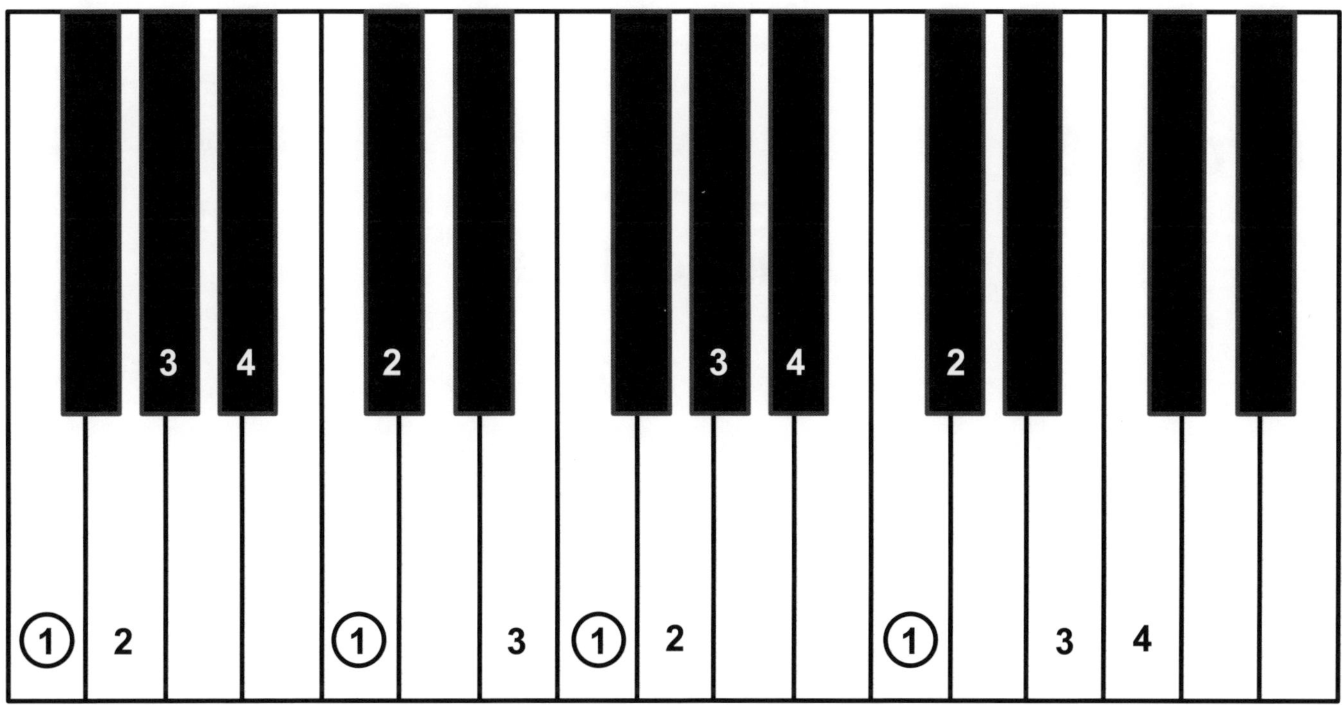

Thumbs on C and F

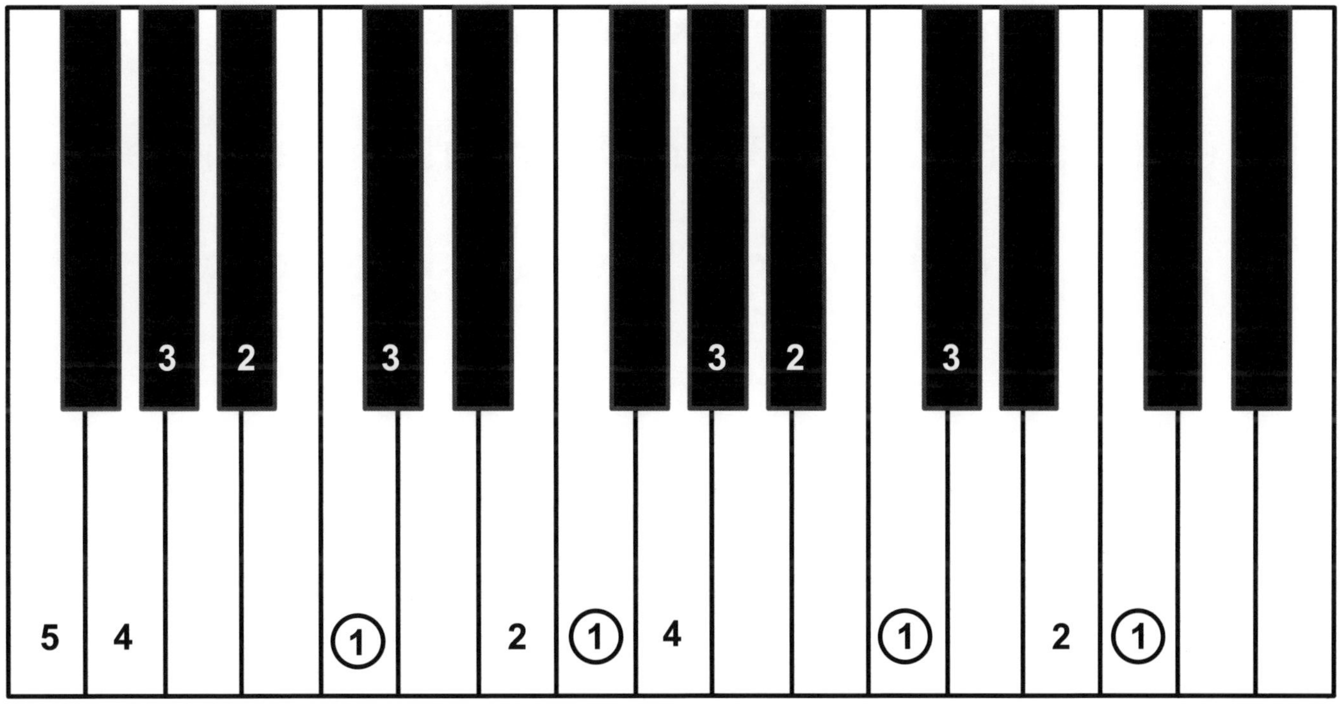

Group 4
F Minor Scale
LH PLAY THE CHORD

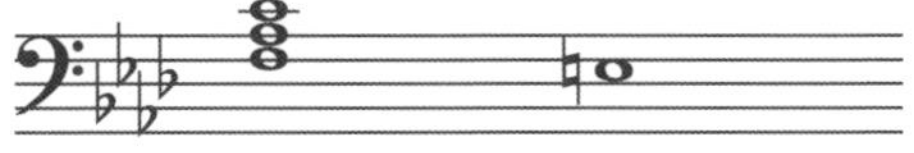

Scales

Group 5

All are different

B minor	Eb minor
Bb minor	F# minor

Tips:

- Compare LH and RH fingers in each keyboard diagram
- Notice which fingers play black notes/white notes

For example: F# minor - 3rd and 4th fingers on black notes

Thumbs and 2nd fingers on white notes

Group 5
B Minor Scale
RH PLAY THE CHORD

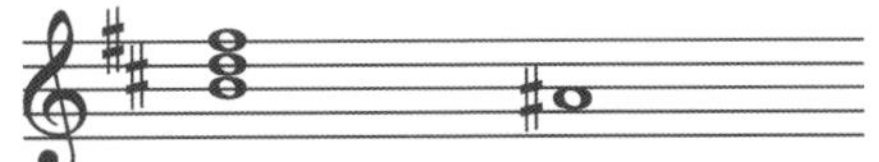

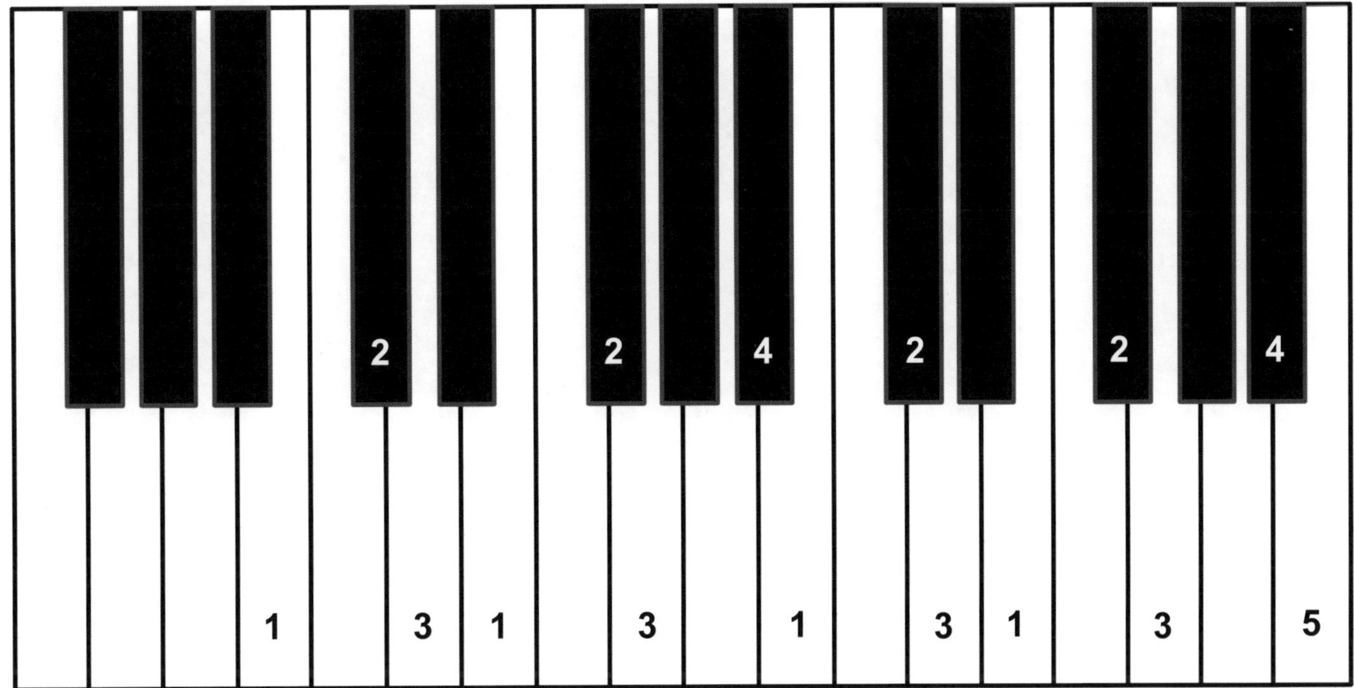

Compare fingering on white and black notes

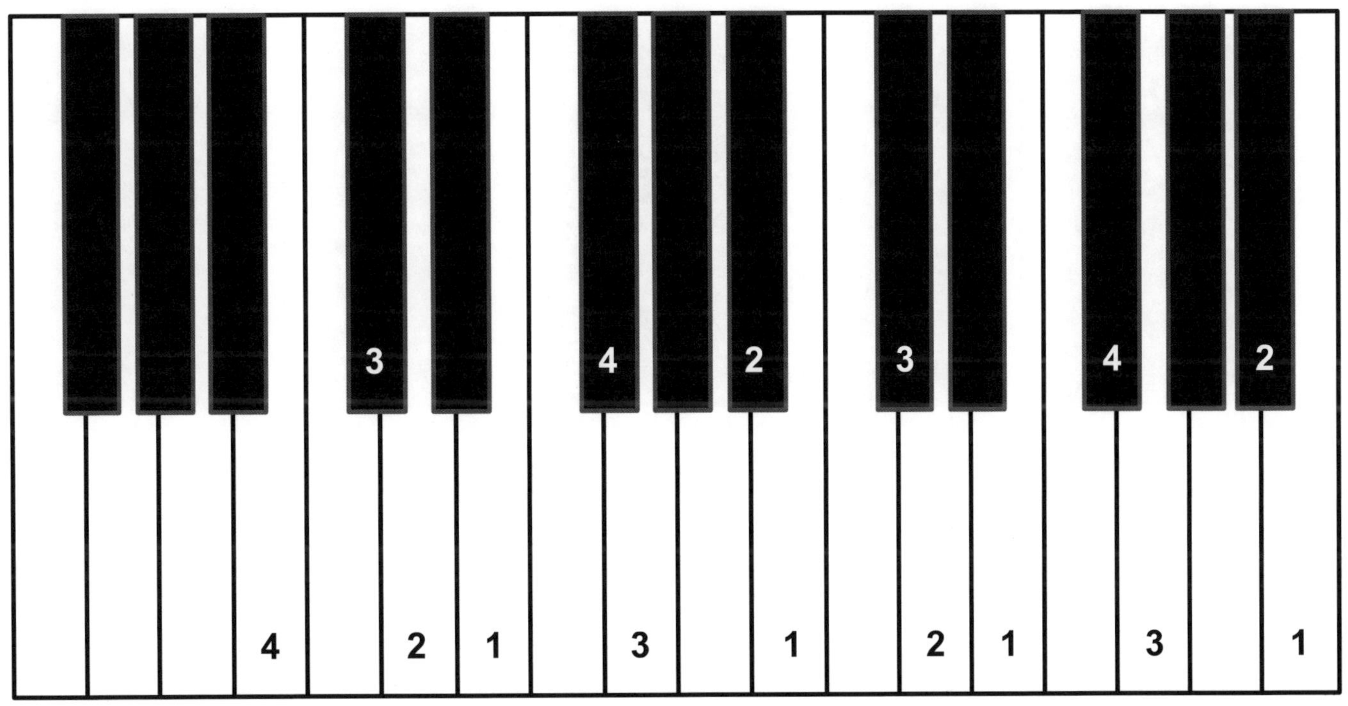

Group 5
B Minor Scale
LH PLAY THE CHORD

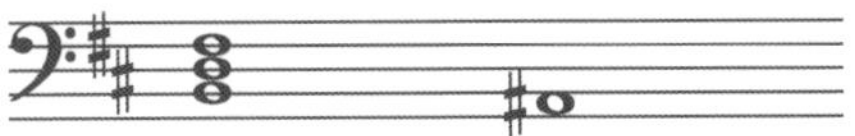

Group 5
Bb Minor Scale
RH PLAY THE CHORD

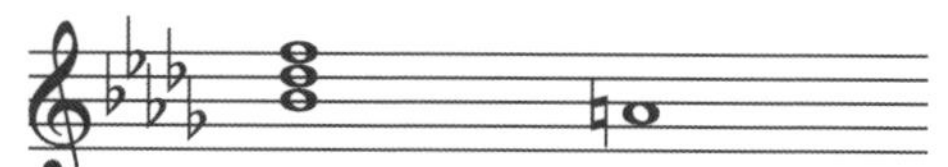

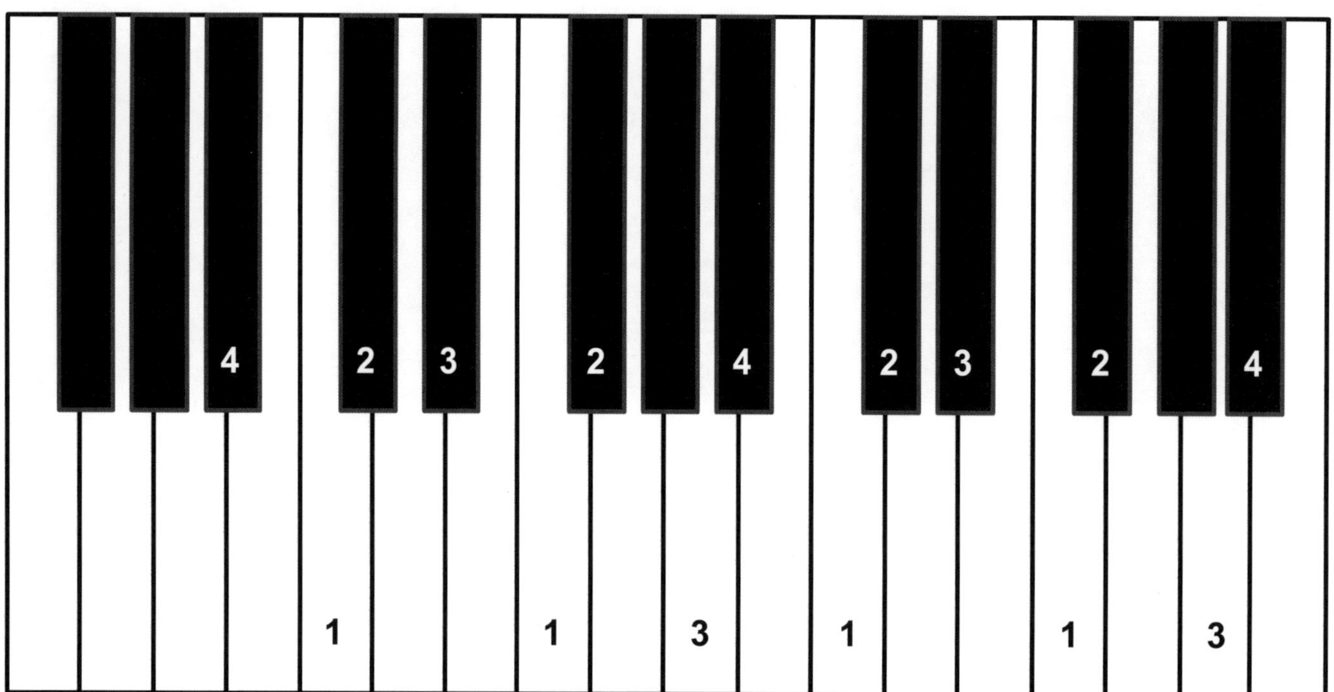

Compare fingering on white and black notes

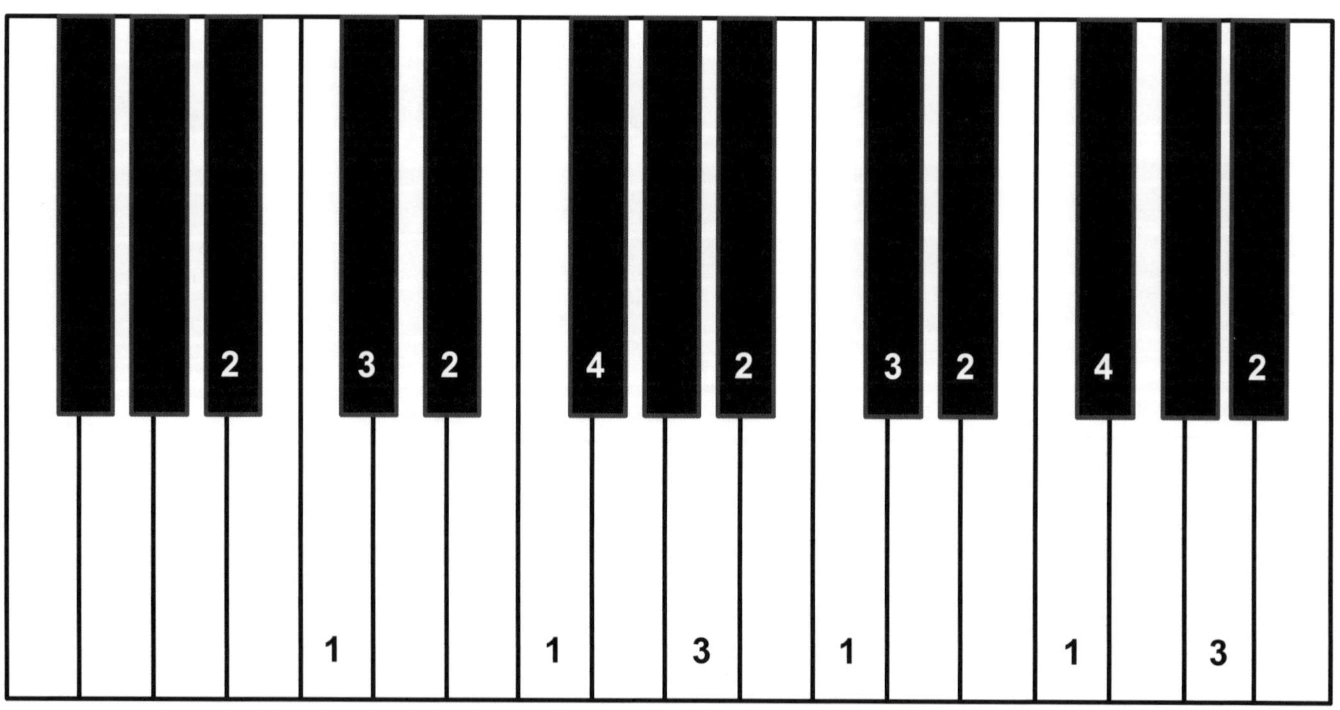

Group 5
Bb Minor Scale
LH PLAY THE CHORD

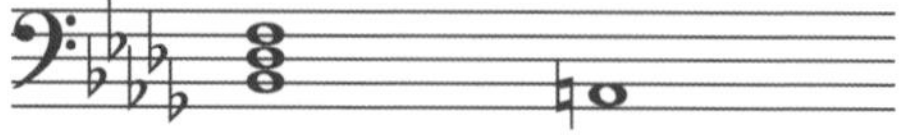

Group 5
Eb Minor Scale
RH PLAY THE CHORD

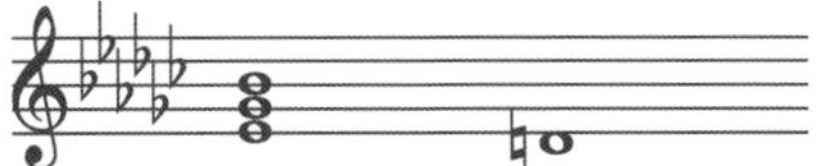

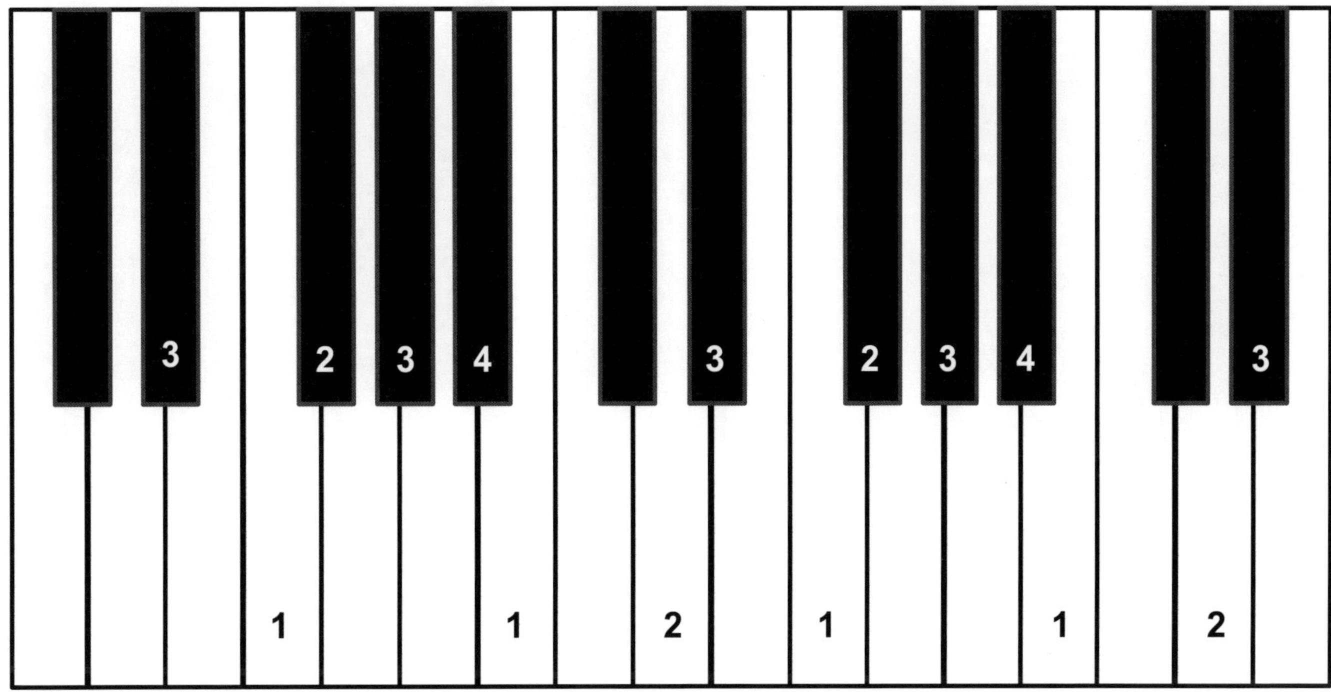

Compare fingering on white and black notes

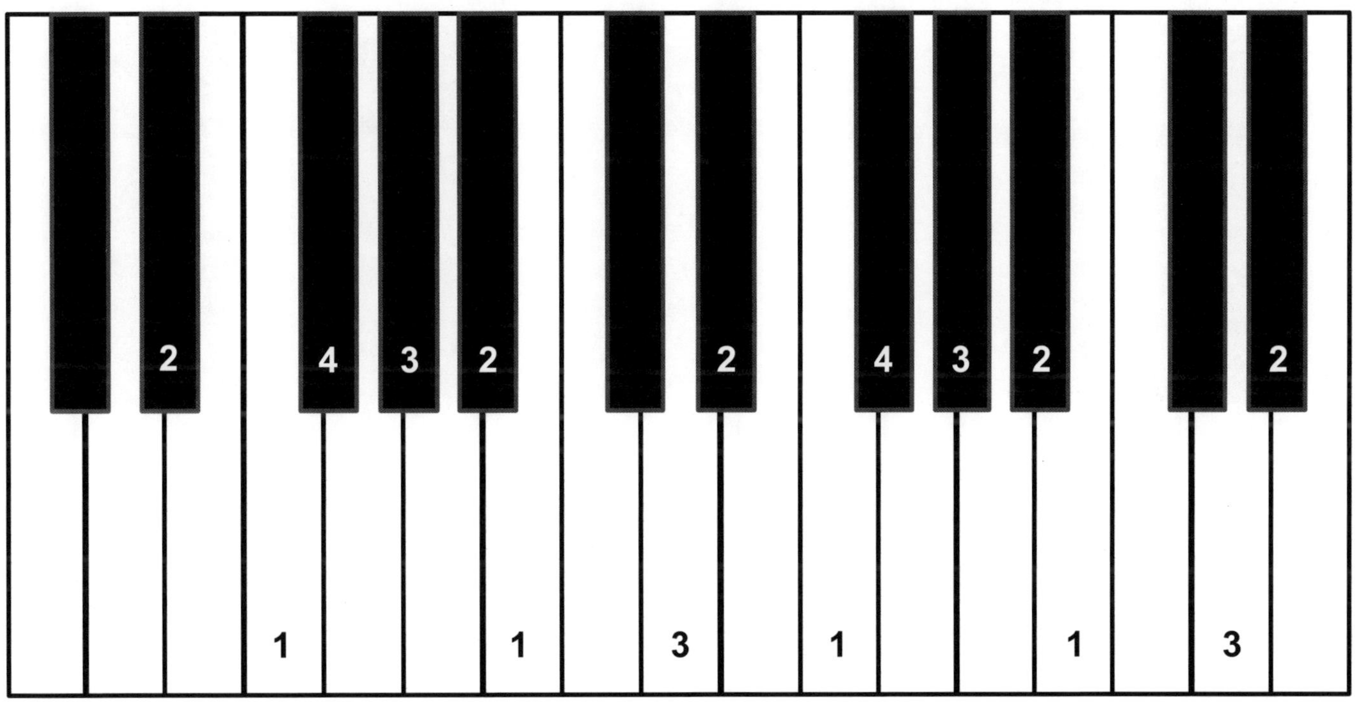

Group 5
Eb Minor Scale
LH PLAY THE CHORD

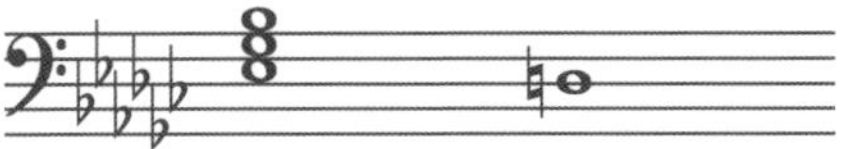

Group 5
F# Minor Scale
RH PLAY THE CHORD

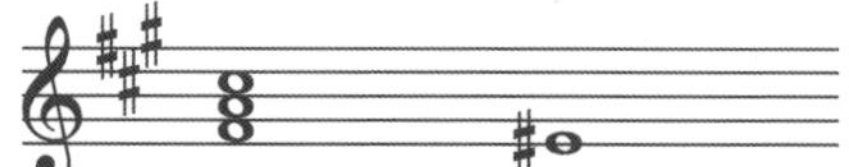

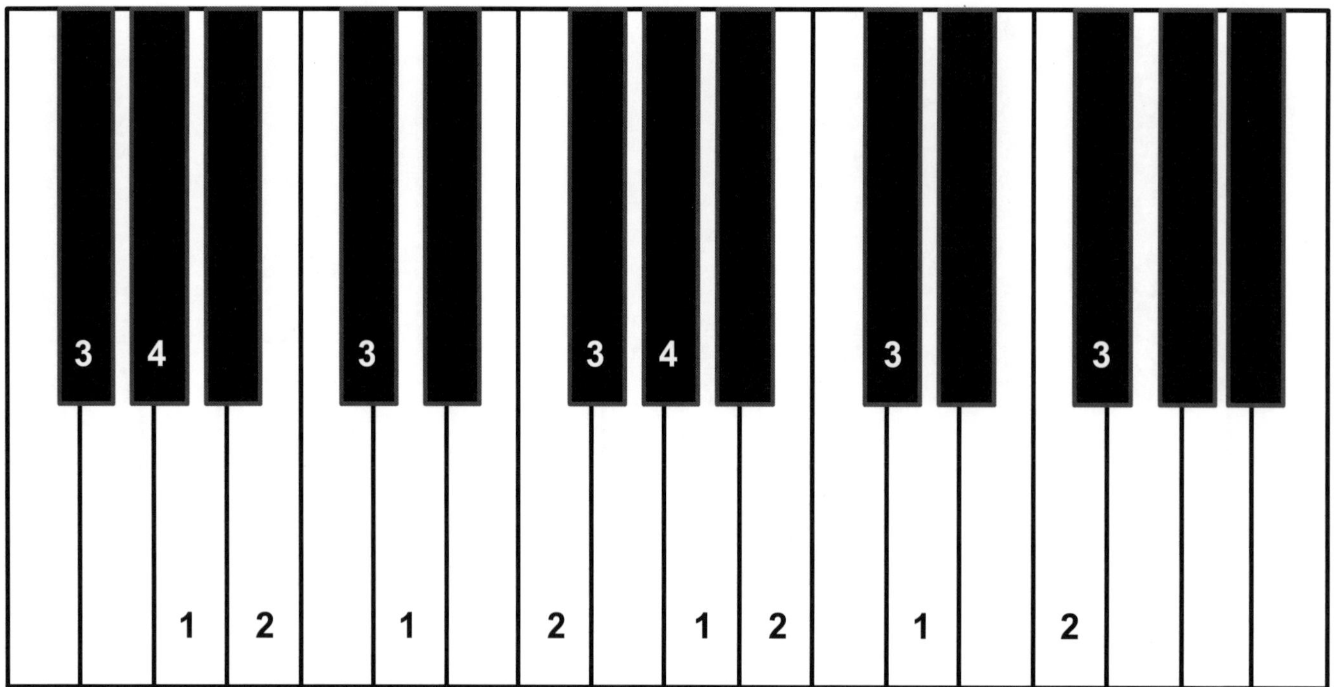

Compare fingering on white and black notes

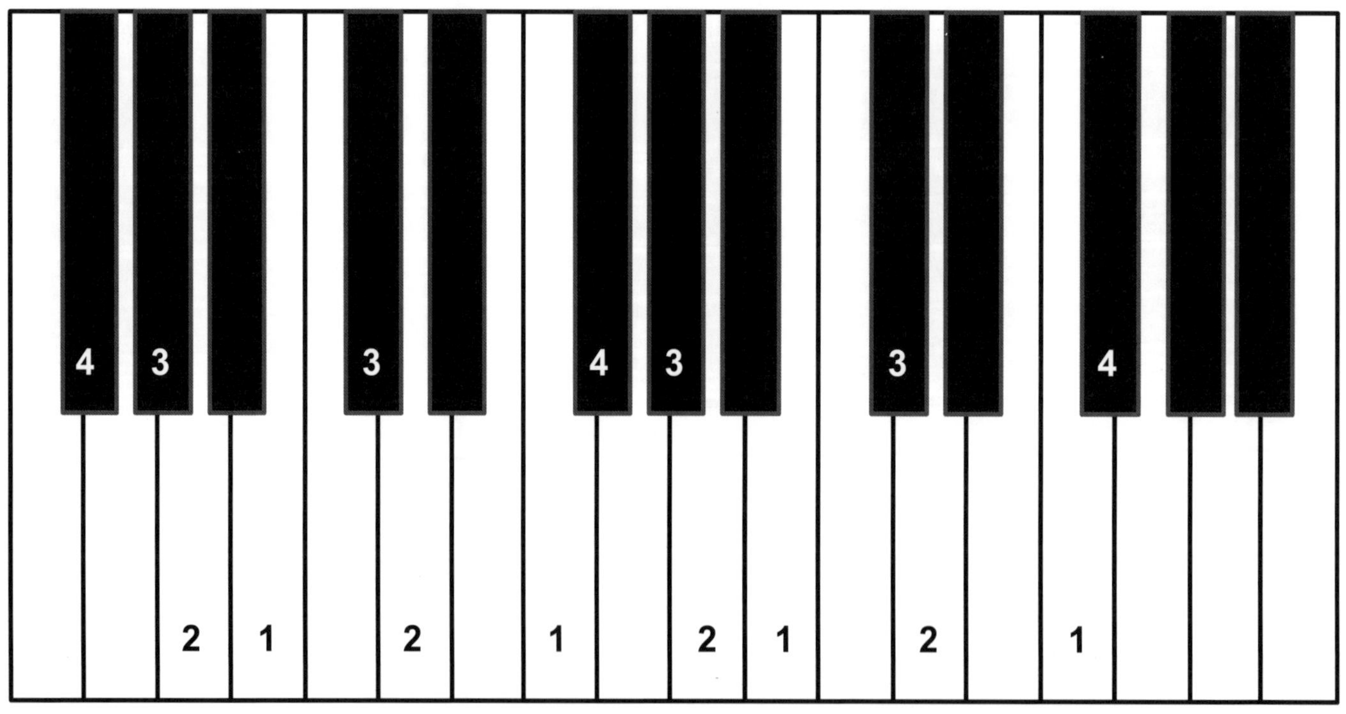

Group 5
F# Minor Scale
LH PLAY THE CHORD

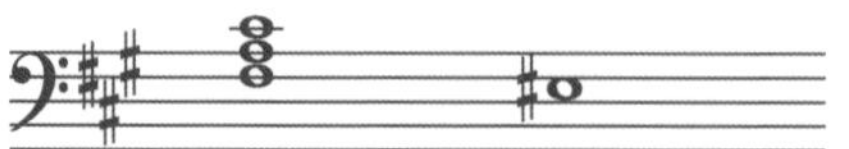

The Arpeggio Groups

Group 1

C major	A minor	F# major
G major	D minor	Eb minor
D major	E minor	B major
A major	F minor	B minor
E major	C minor	
F major	G minor	

Group 2

Eb major	G# minor	C# minor
Ab major	Db major	F# minor

Group 3

Bb major	Bb minor

Play the chord first EVERY time

Say the note names as you play for clarity.

Remember:

C major chord:	C	E	G
C minor chord:	C	Eb	G

The middle note in a minor chord is a semitone down from the major chord.

Arpeggios

Group 1

Rule: No 4th fingers

All white notes

C major	D minor
G major	A minor
F major	E minor

One black note

D major	C minor
A major	G minor
E major	F minor

Odd

B major	B minor

All black notes

F# major	Eb minor

Group 1

C Major Arpeggio

RH PLAY THE CHORD

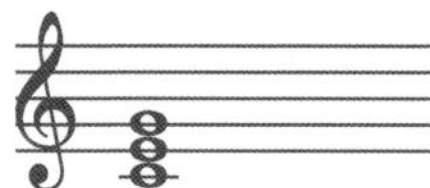

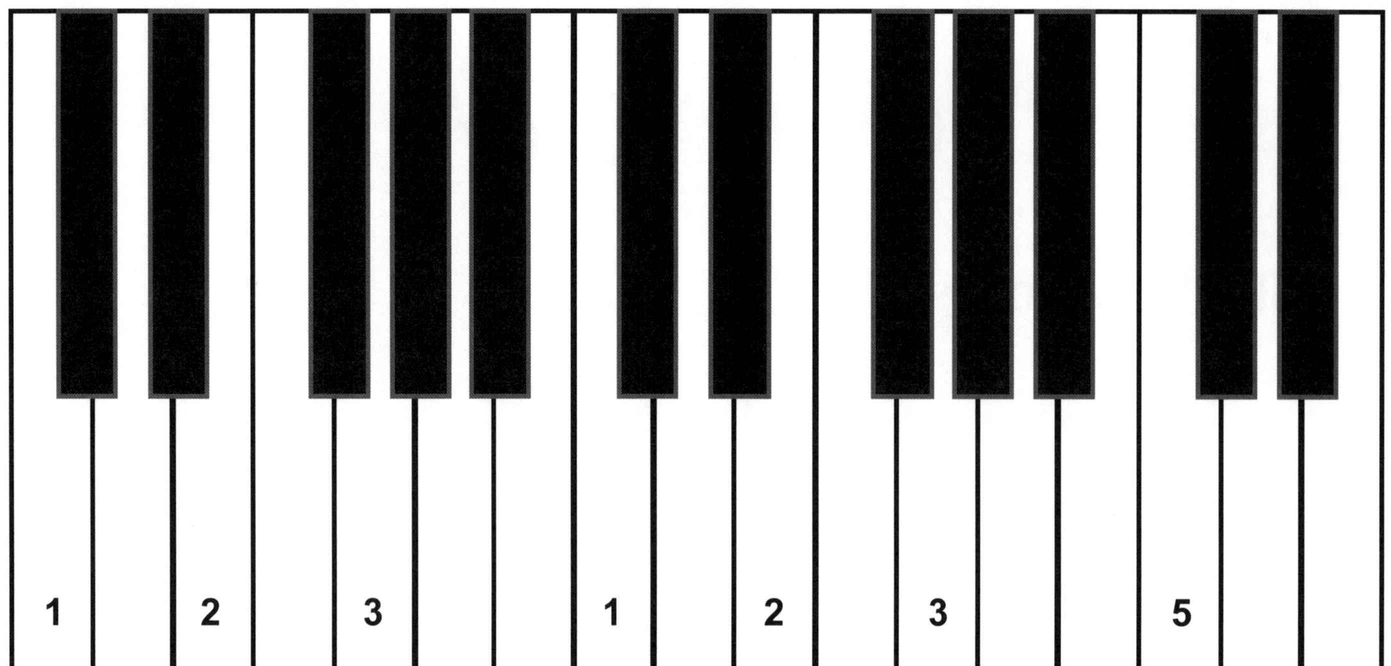

All white notes

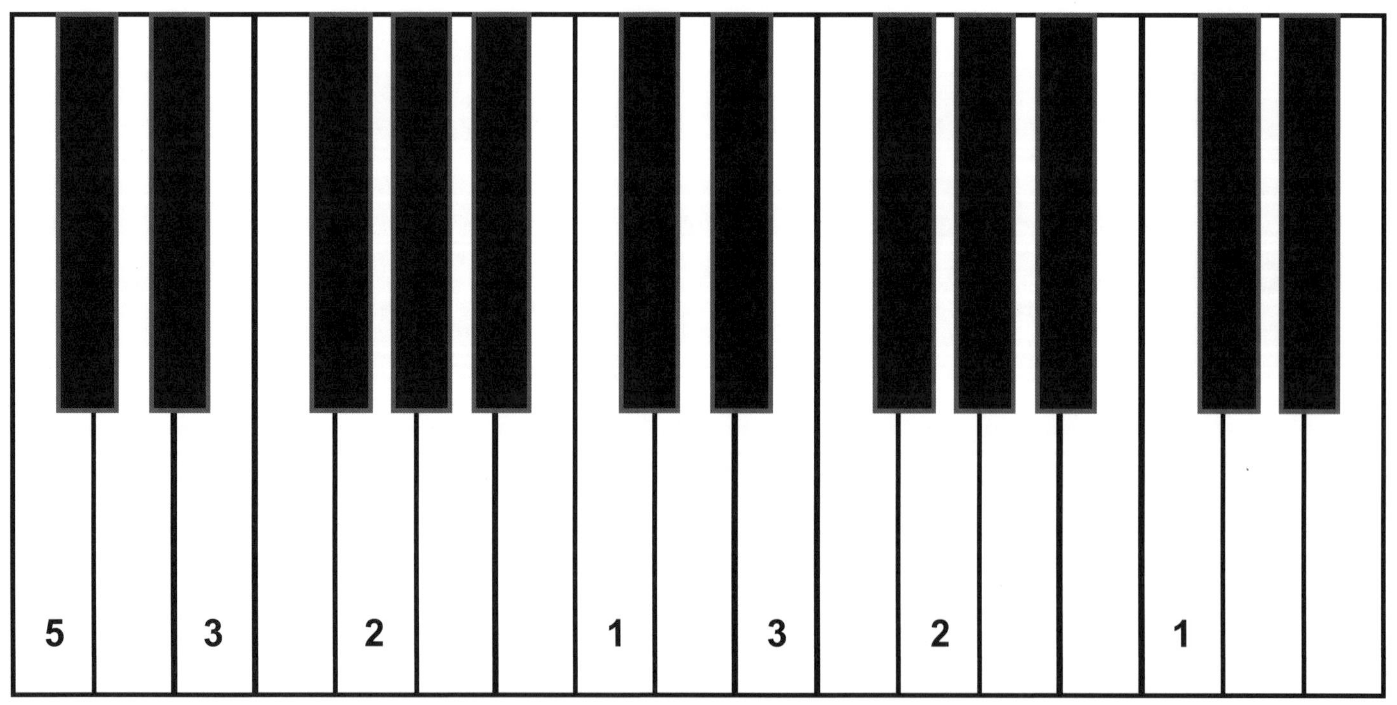

Group 1

C Major Arpeggio

LH PLAY THE CHORD

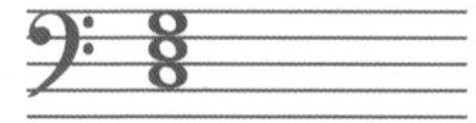

Group 1
G Major Arpeggio
RH PLAY THE CHORD

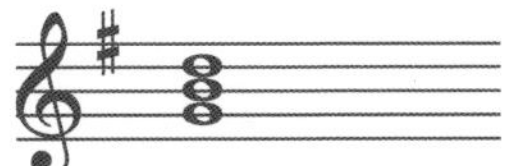

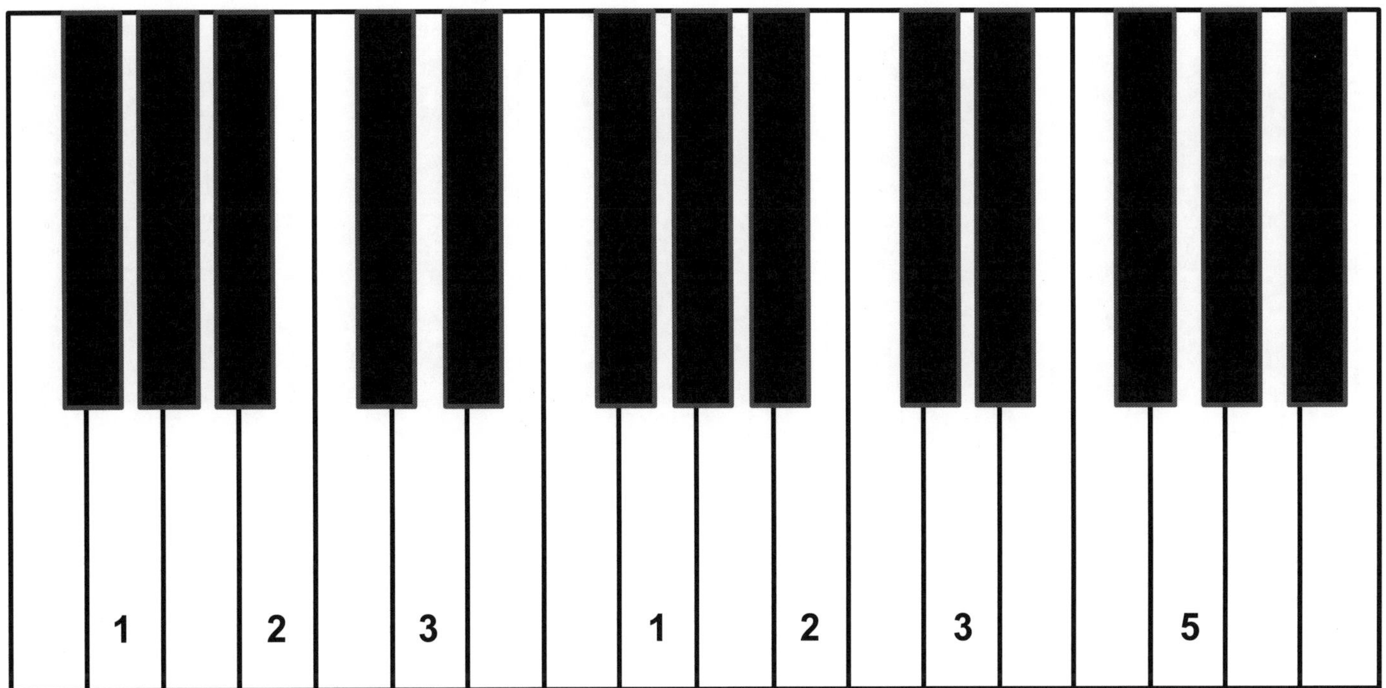

All white notes

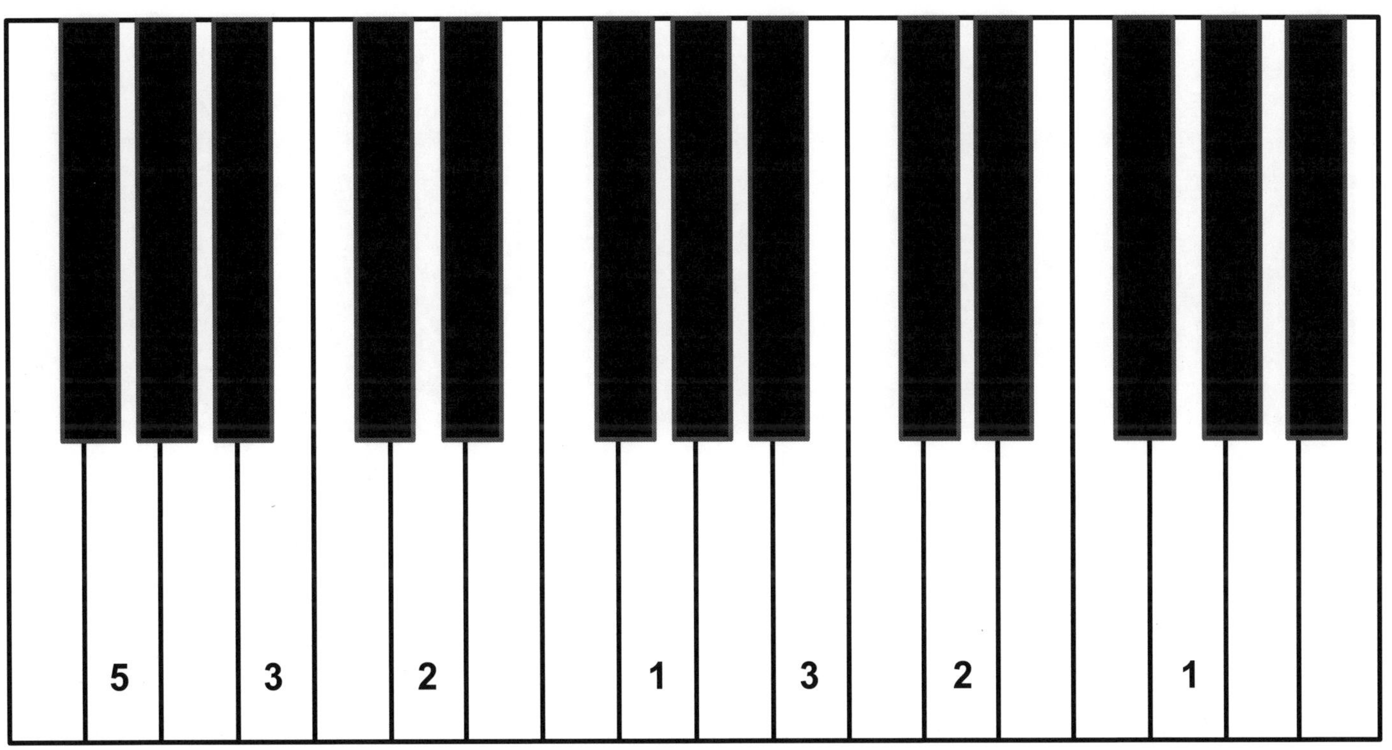

Group 1
G Major Arpeggio
LH PLAY THE CHORD

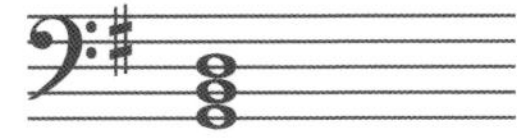

Group 1

F Major Arpeggio

RH PLAY THE CHORD

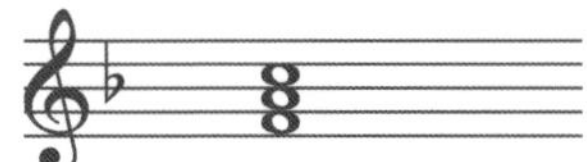

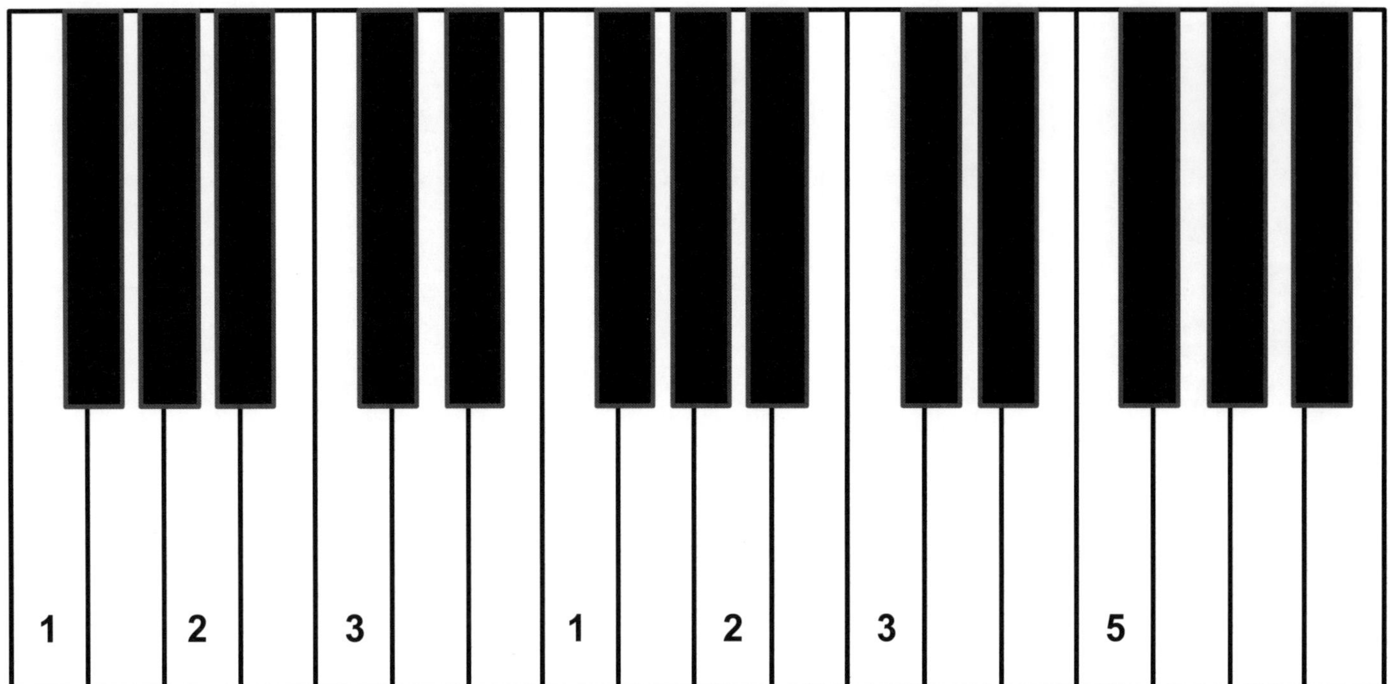

All white notes

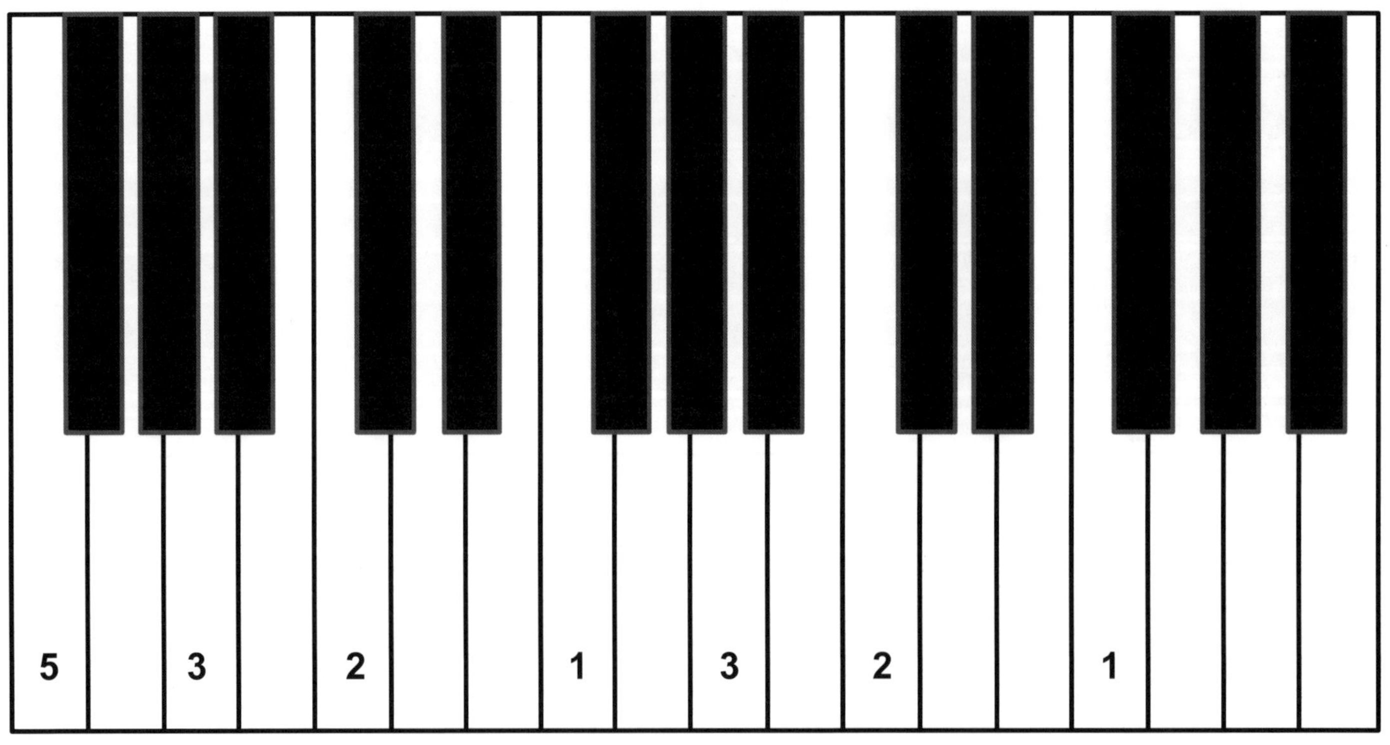

Group 1

F Major Arpeggio

LH PLAY THE CHORD

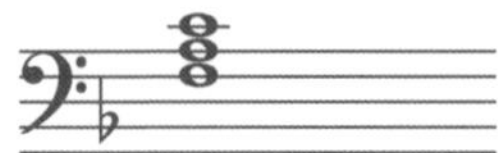

Group 1

D Minor Arpeggio

RH PLAY THE CHORD

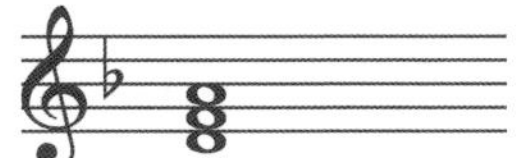

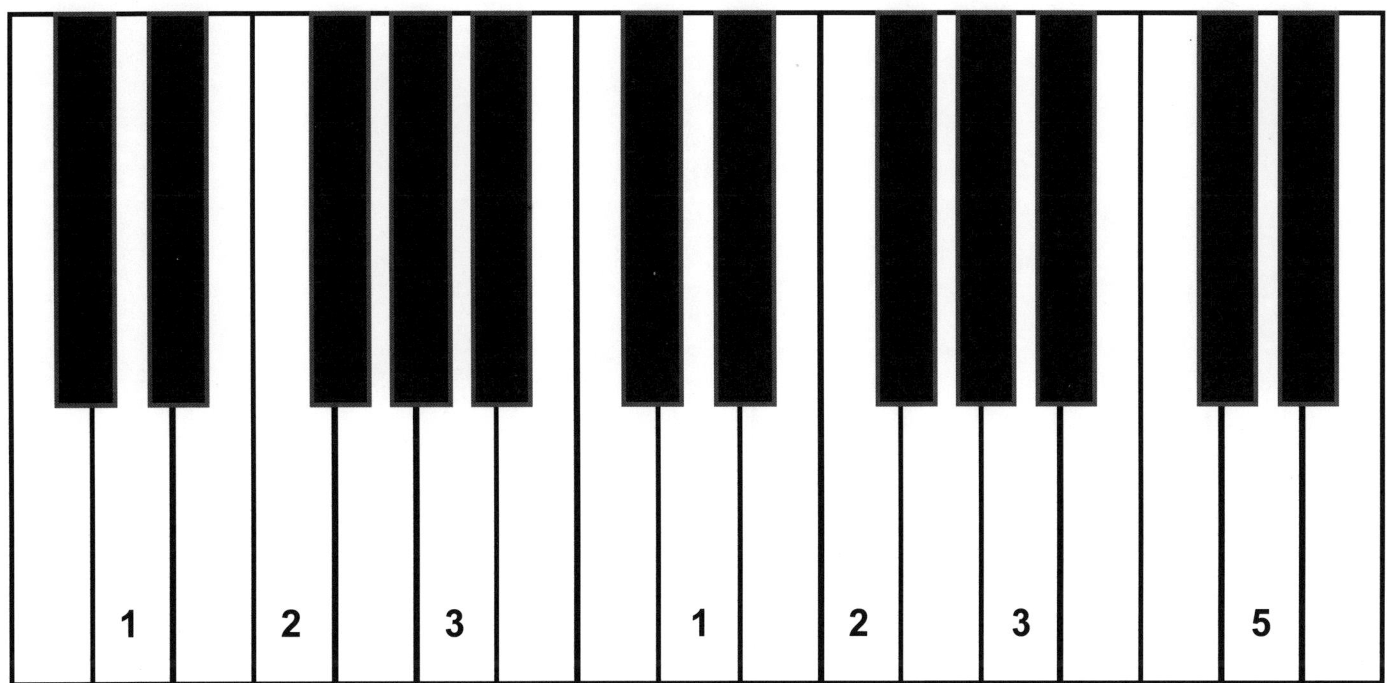

All white notes

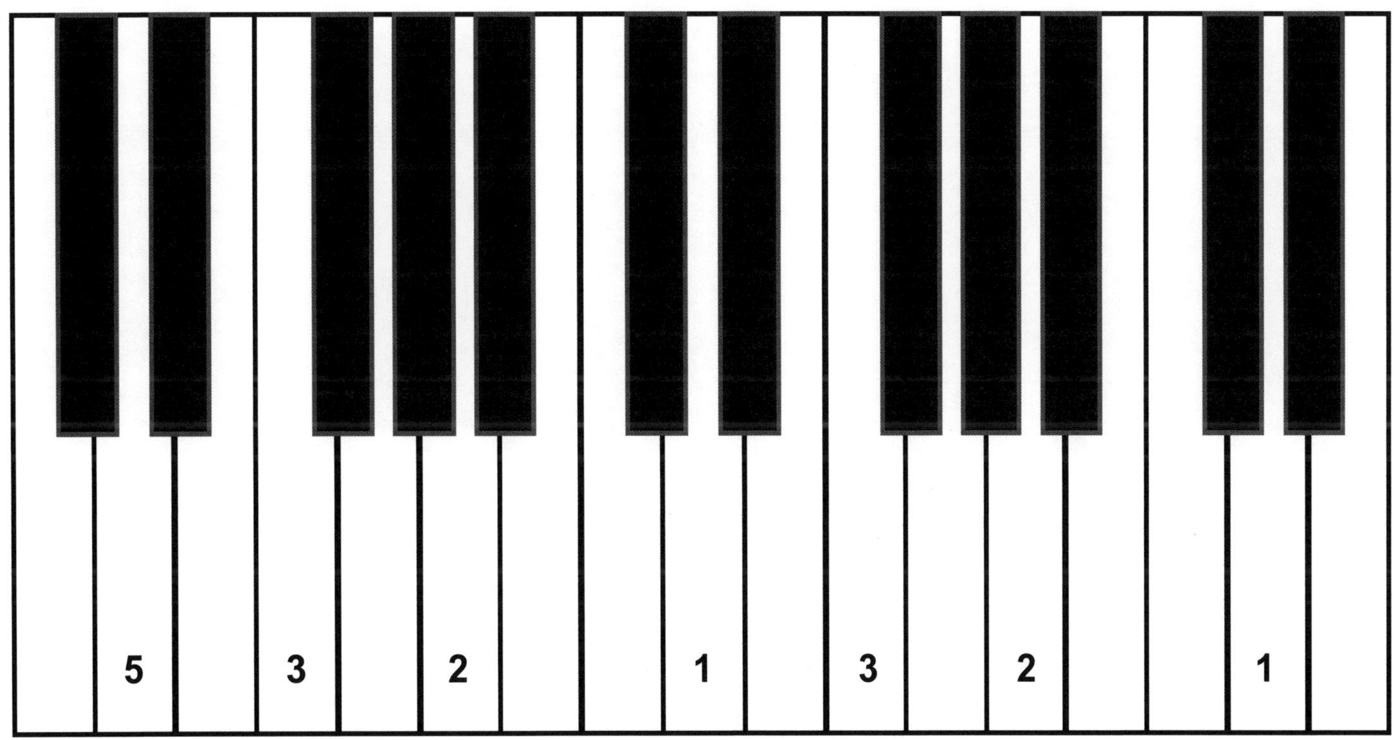

Group 1

D Minor Arpeggio

LH PLAY THE CHORD

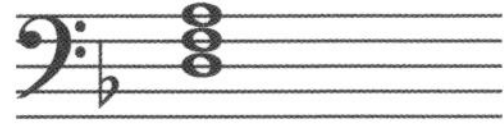

Group 1

A Minor Arpeggio

RH PLAY THE CHORD

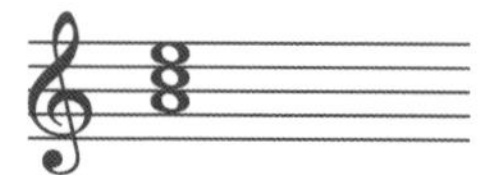

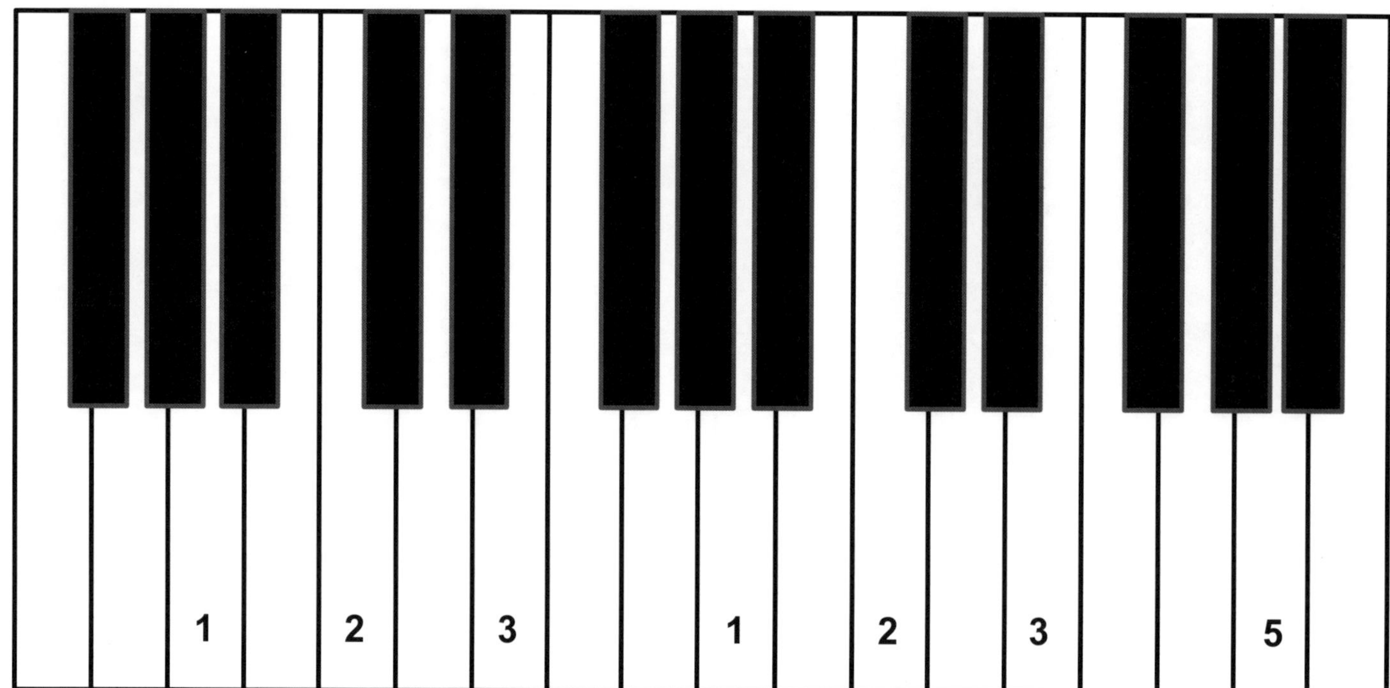

All white notes

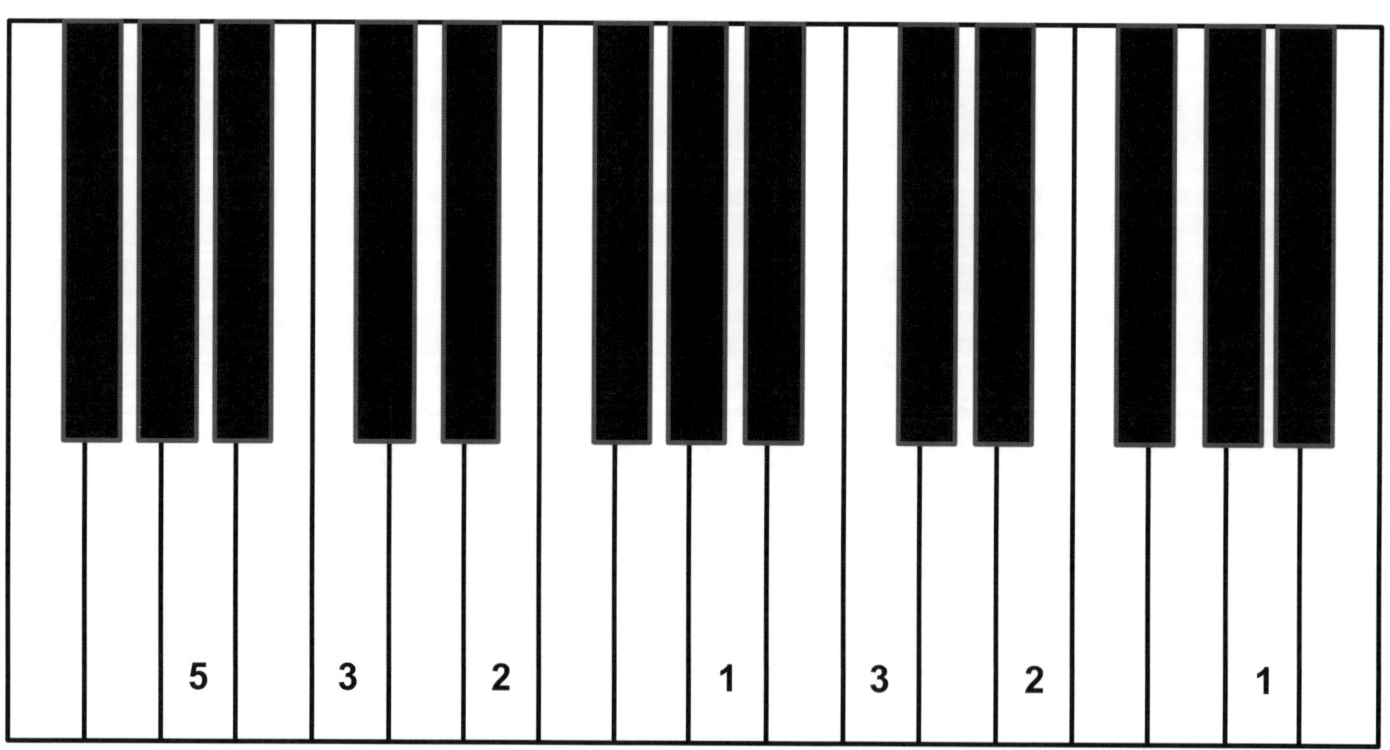

Group 1

A Minor Arpeggio

LH PLAY THE CHORD

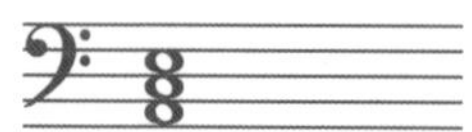

Group 1

E Minor Arpeggio

RH PLAY THE CHORD

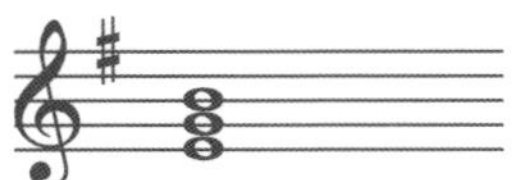

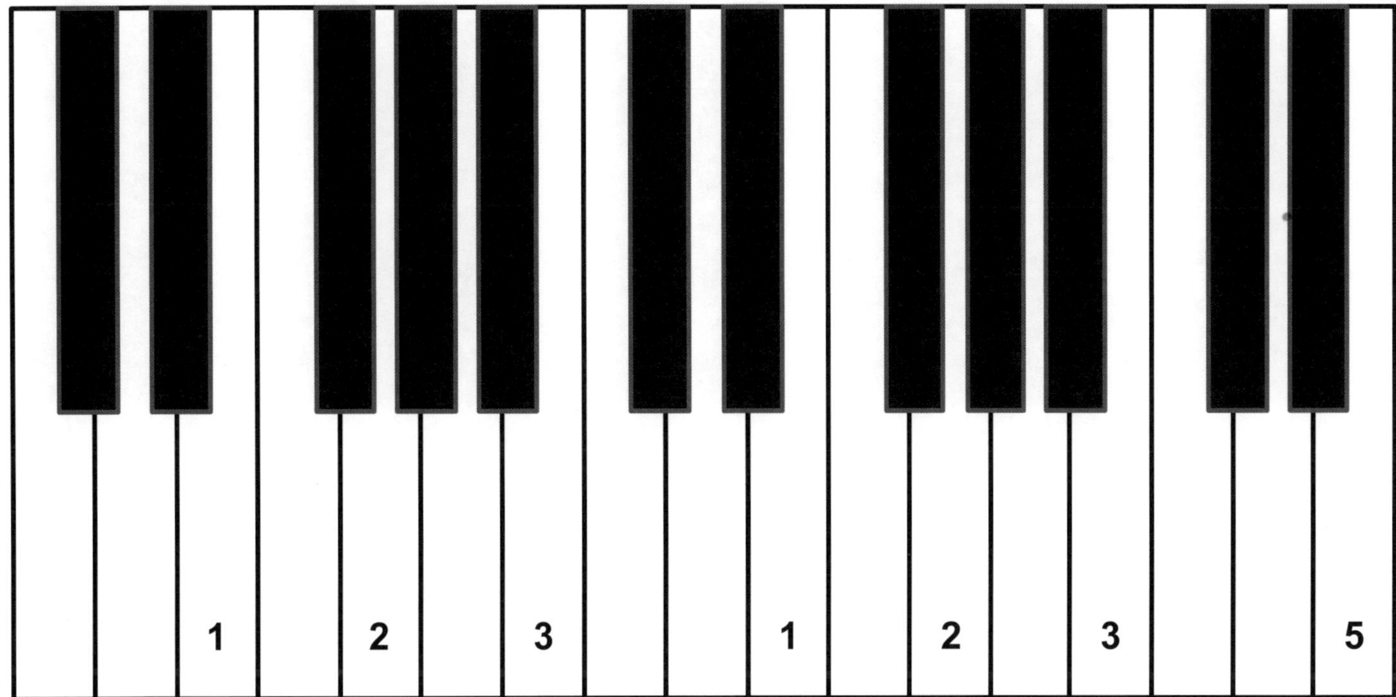

All white notes

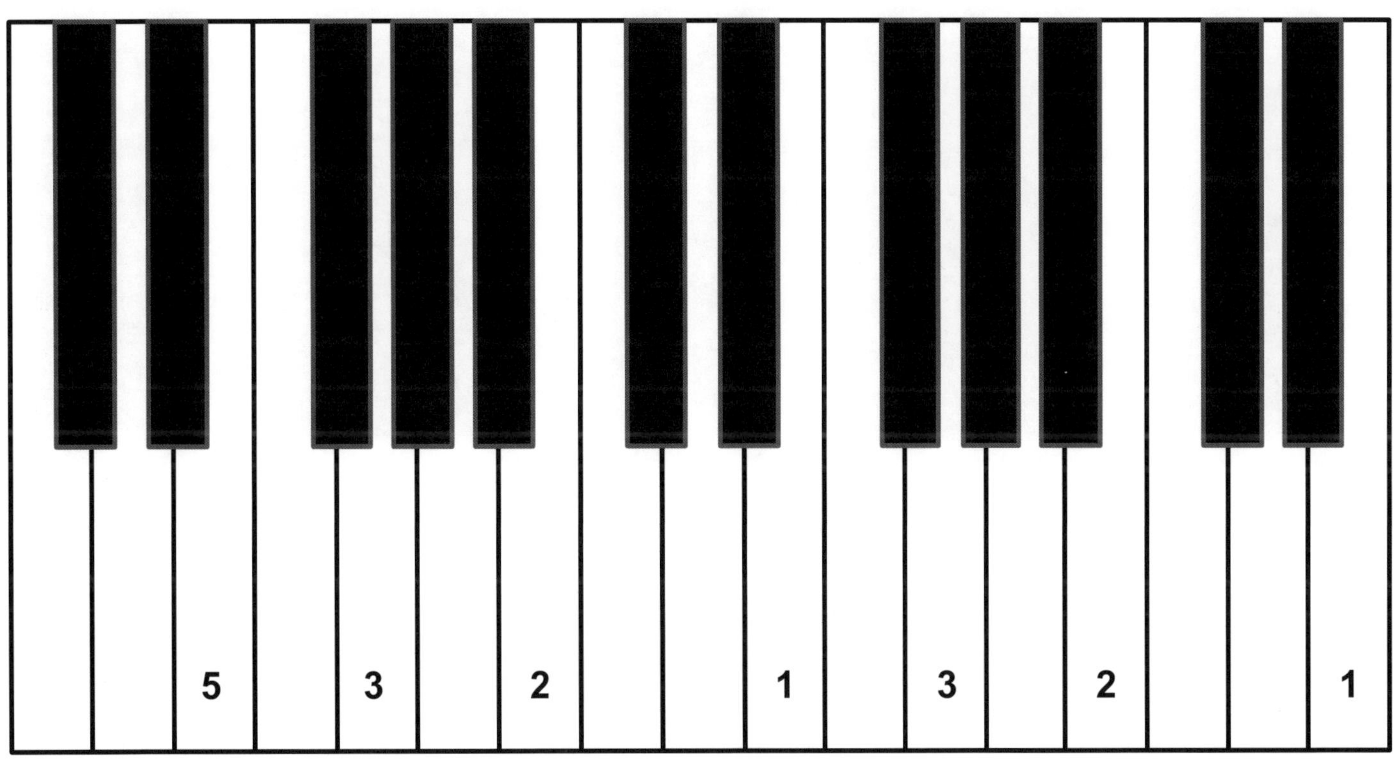

Group 1

E Minor Arpeggio

LH PLAY THE CHORD

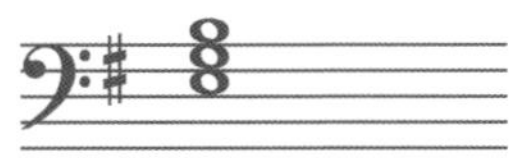

Group 1

D Major Arpeggio

RH PLAY THE CHORD

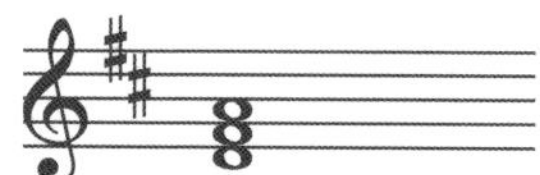

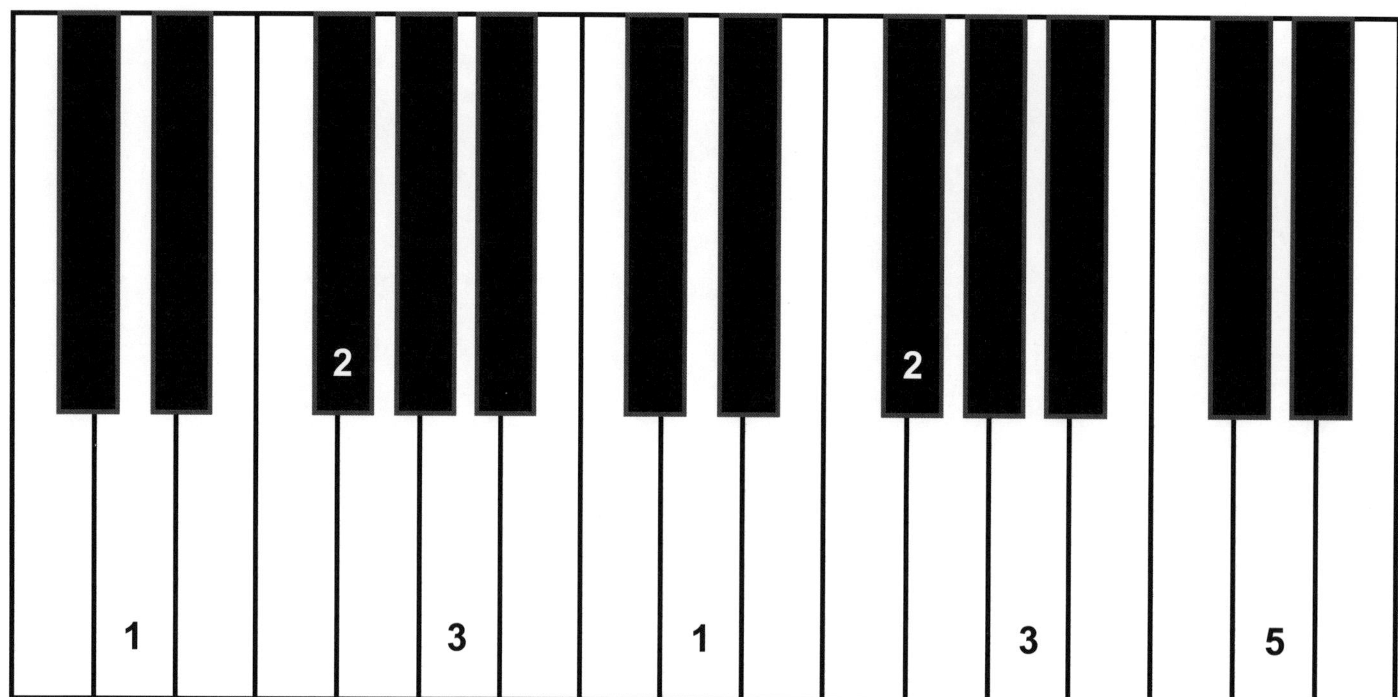

One black note

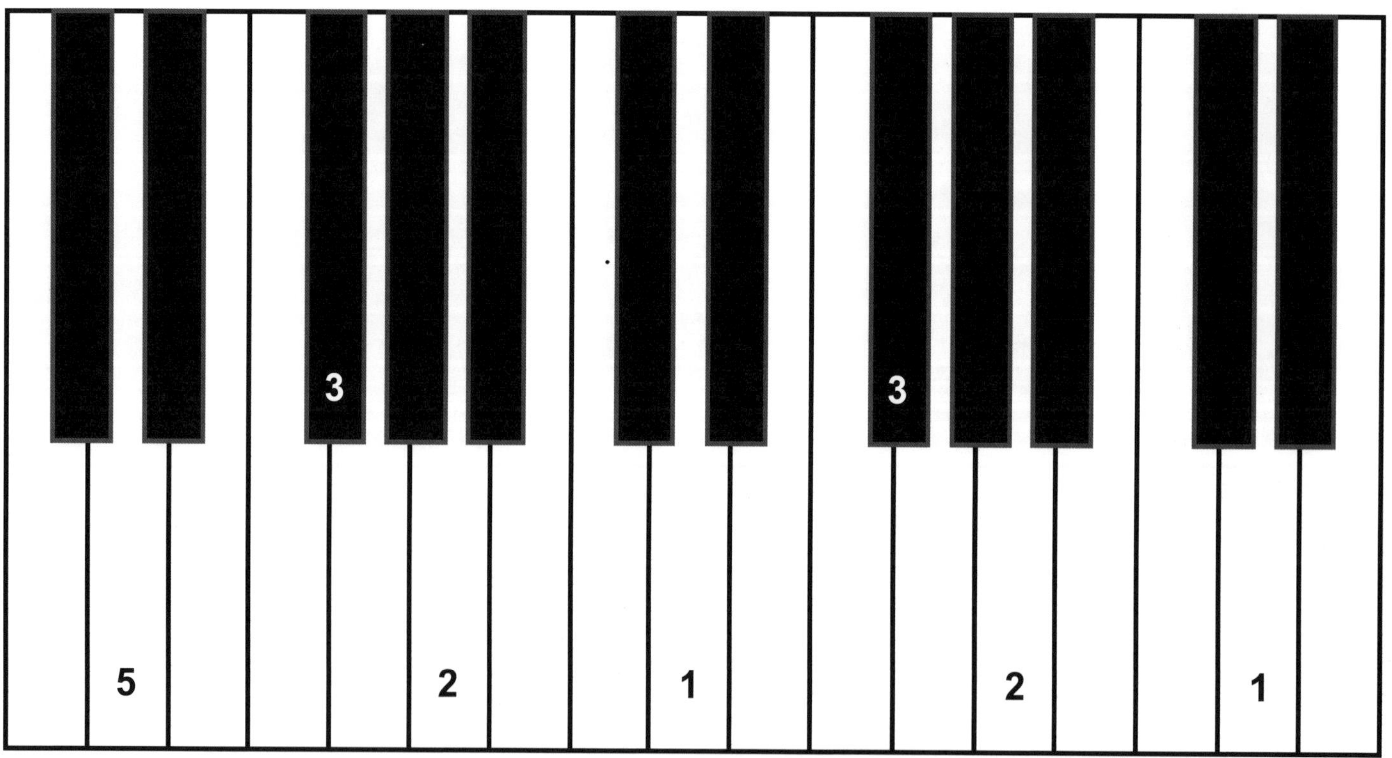

Group 1

D Major Arpeggio

LH PLAY THE CHORD

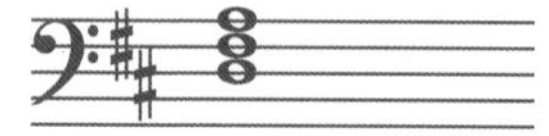

Group 1
A Major Arpeggio
RH PLAY THE CHORD

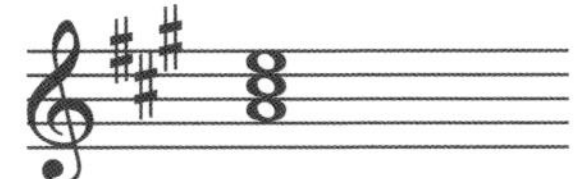

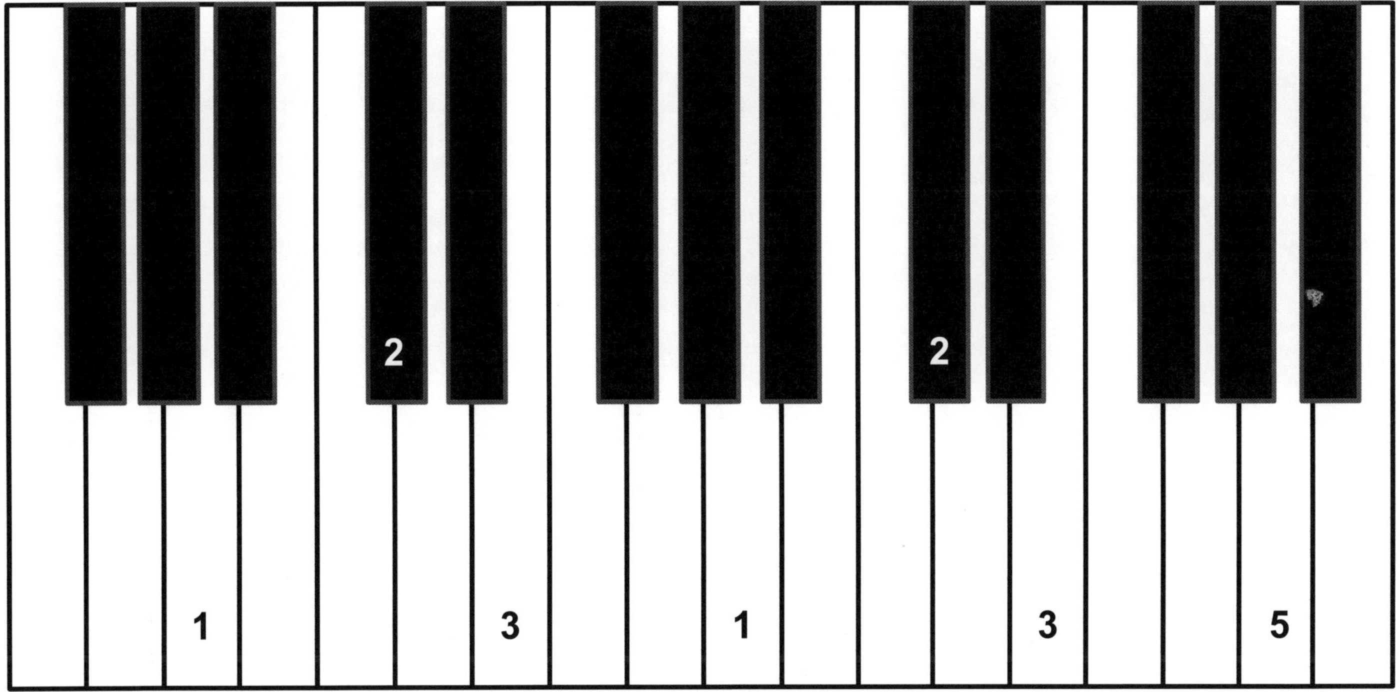

One black note

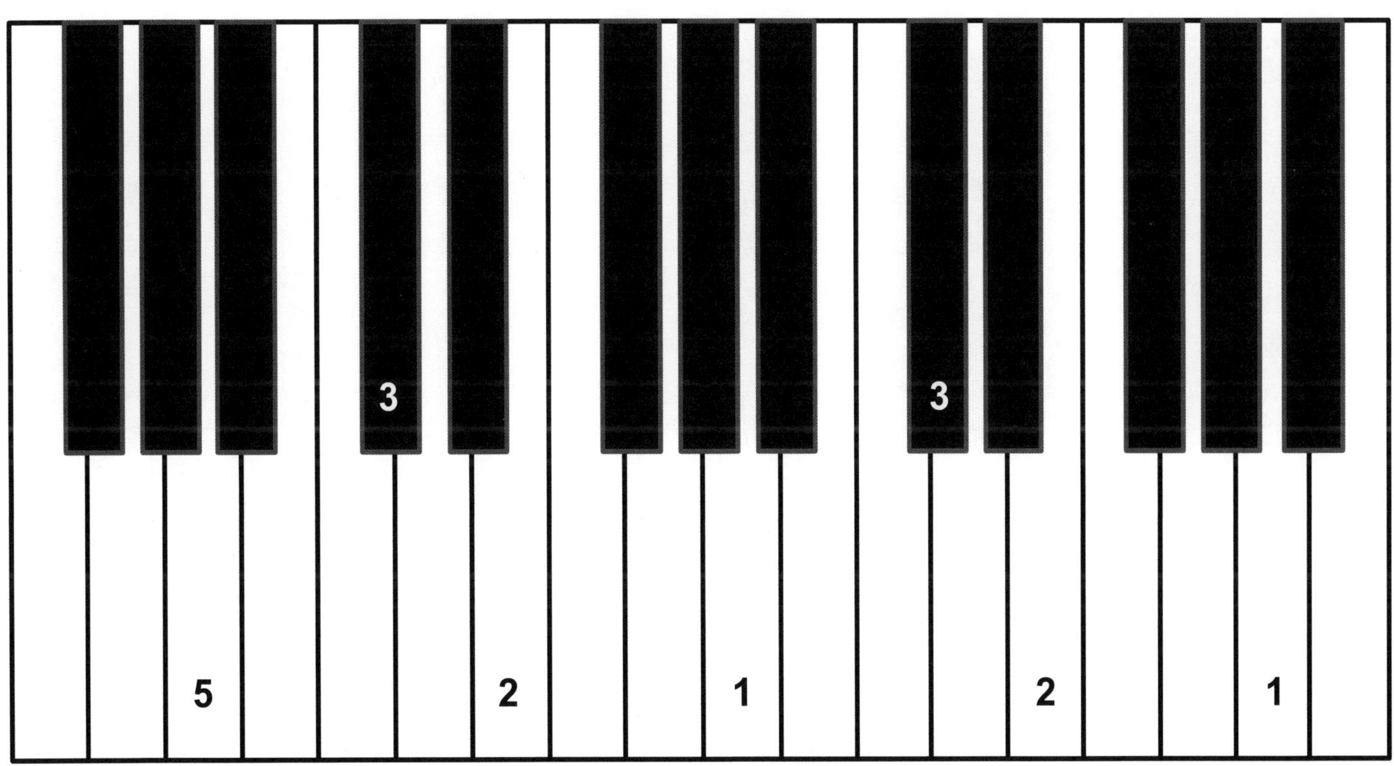

Group 1
A Major Arpeggio
LH PLAY THE CHORD

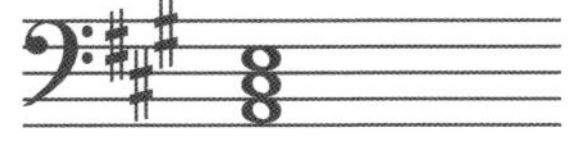

Group 1
E Major Arpeggio
RH PLAY THE CHORD

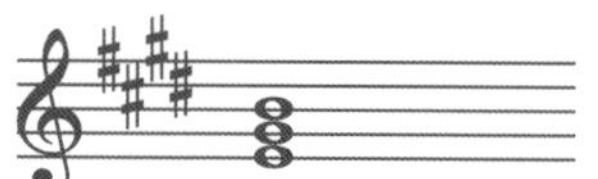

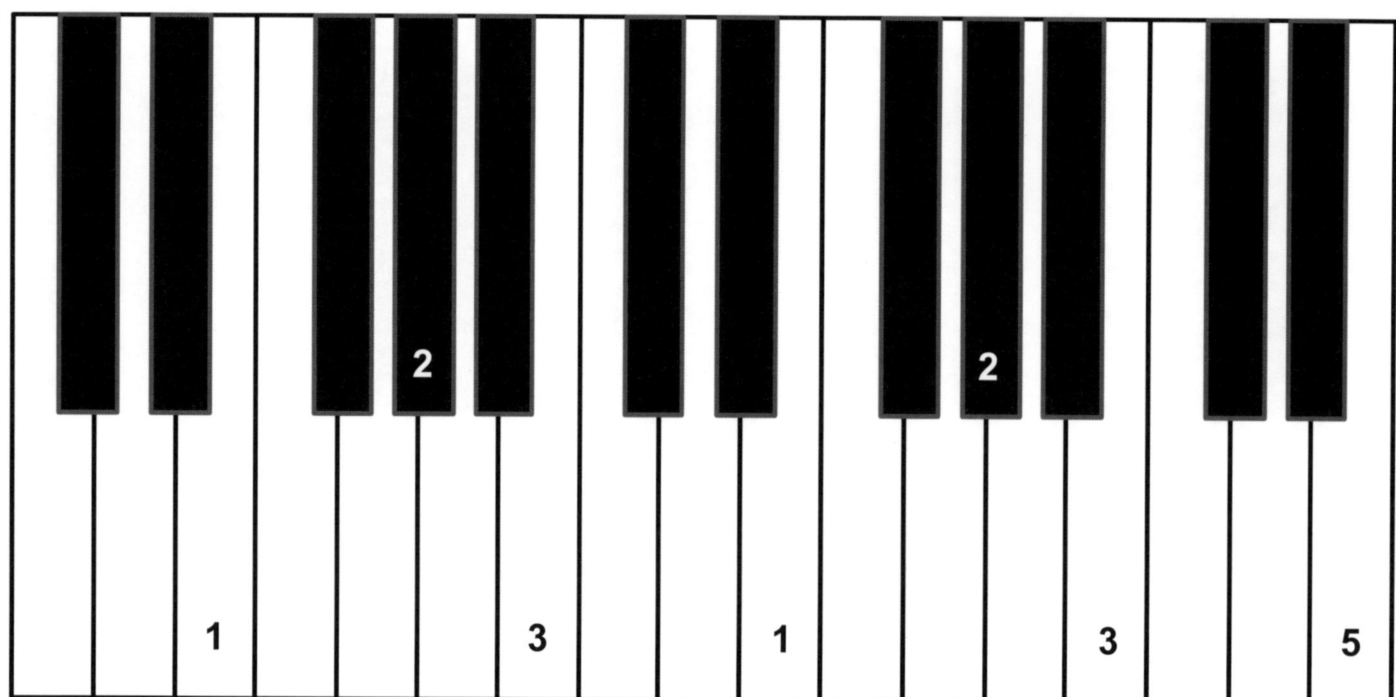

One black note

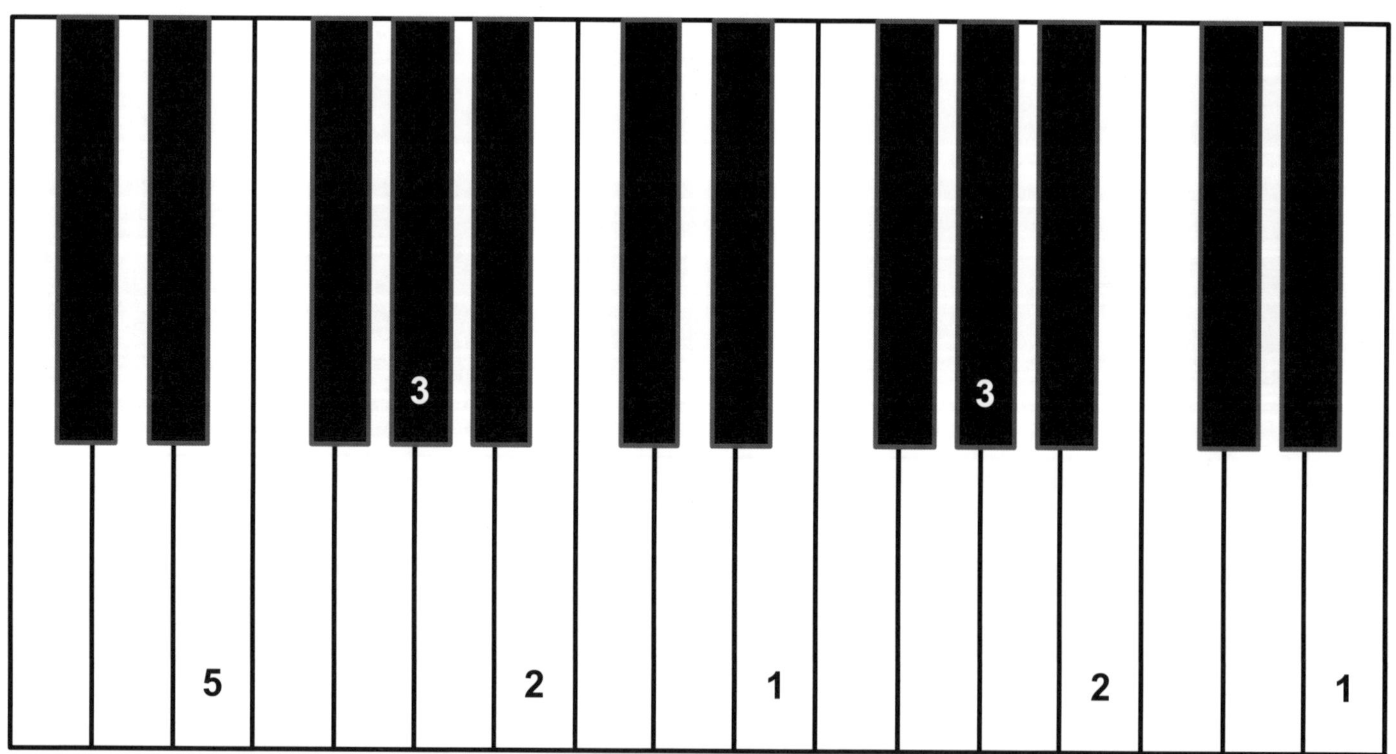

Group 1
E Major Arpeggio
LH PLAY THE CHORD

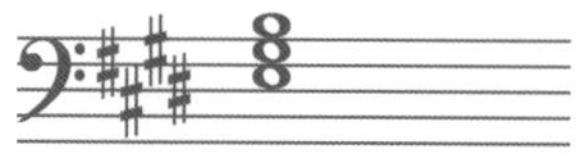

Group 1

C Minor Arpeggio

RH PLAY THE CHORD

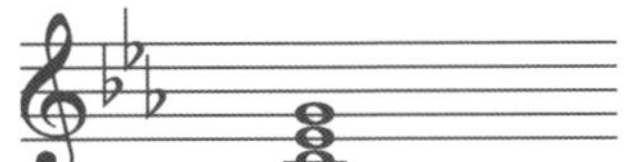

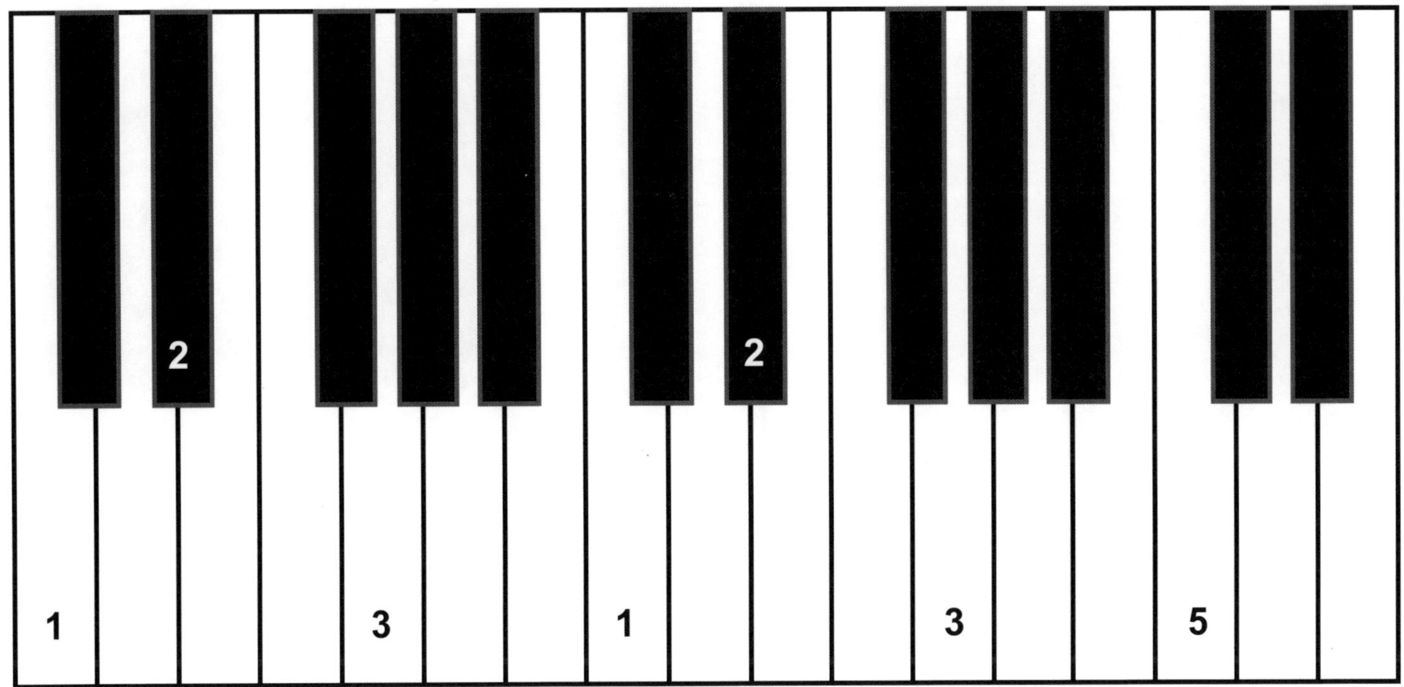

One black note

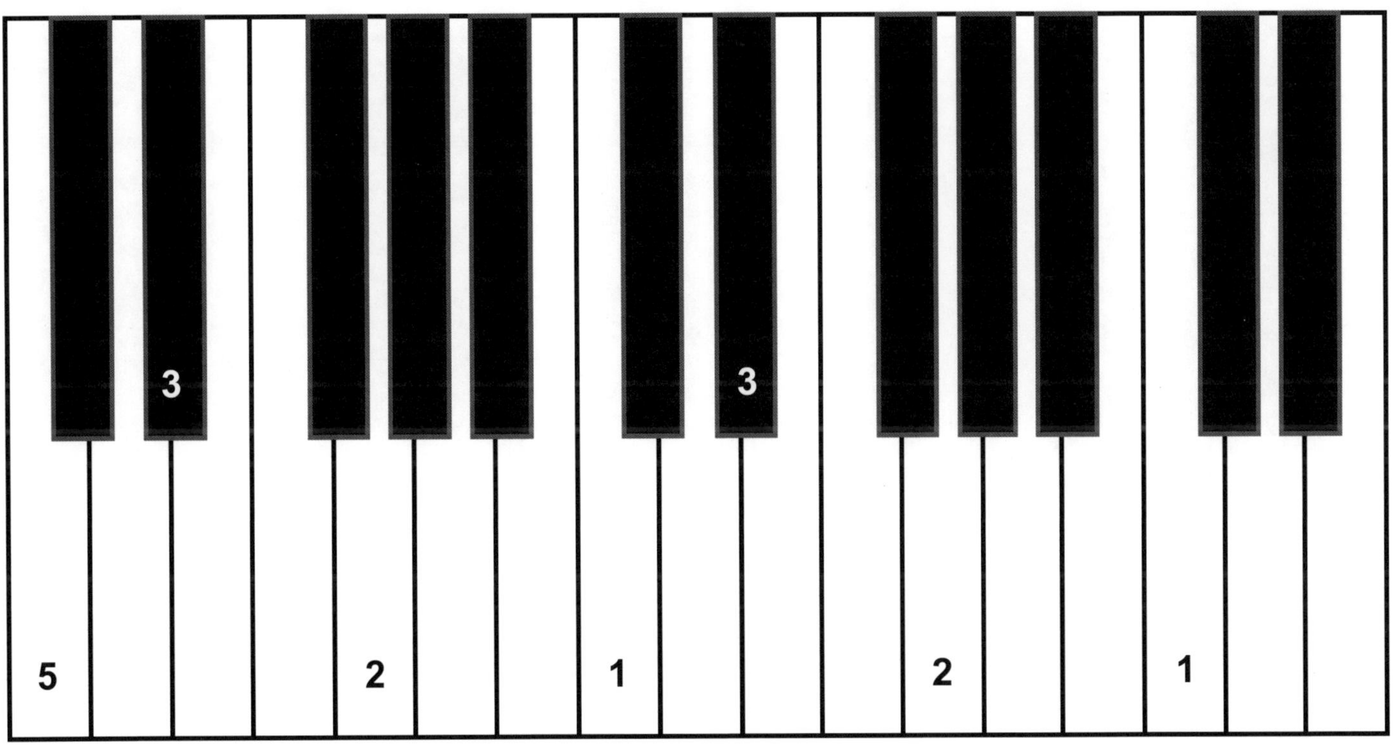

Group 1

C Minor Arpeggio

LH PLAY THE CHORD

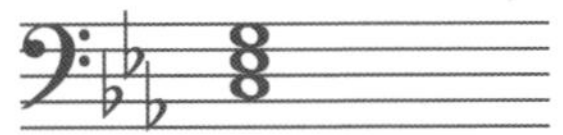

Group 1

G Minor Arpeggio

RH PLAY THE CHORD

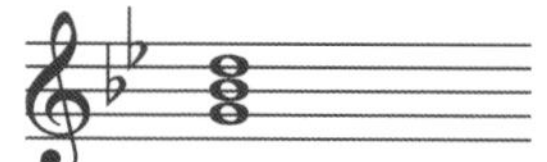

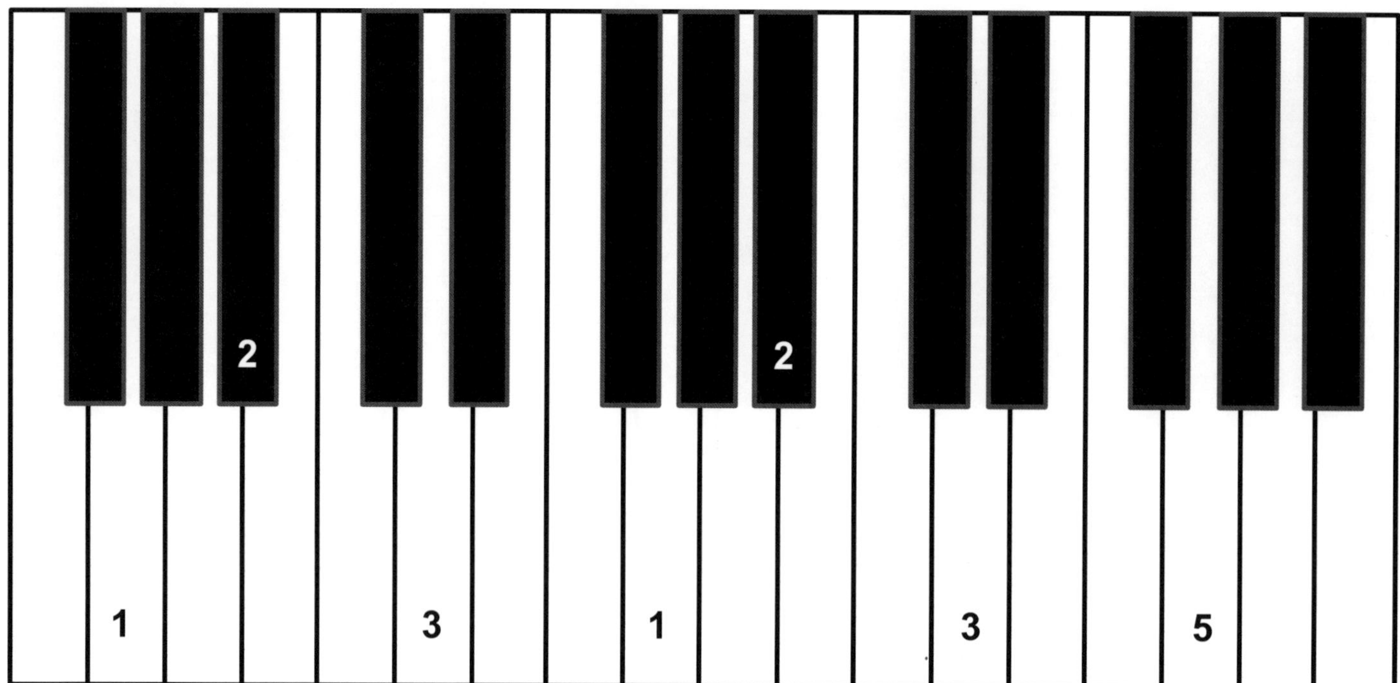

One black note

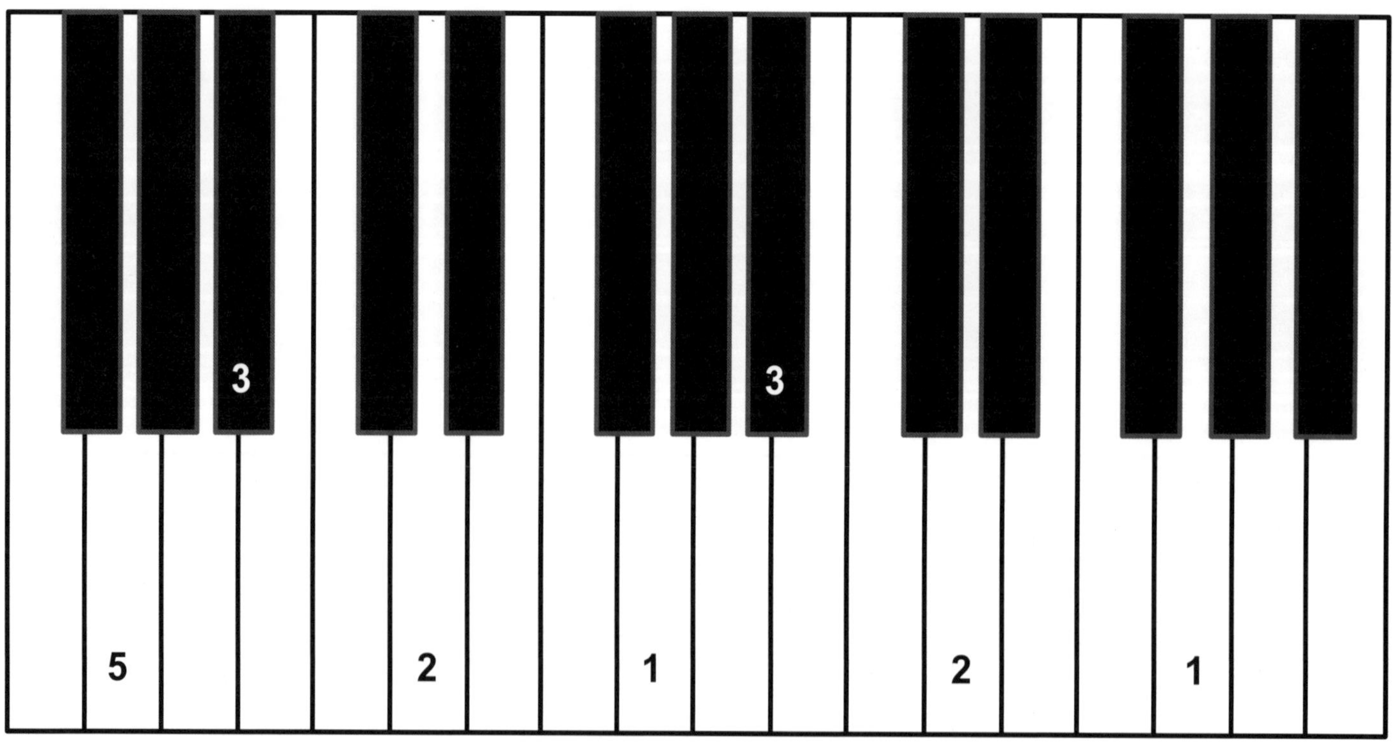

Group 1

G Minor Arpeggio

LH PLAY THE CHORD

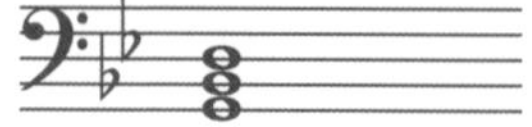

Group 1

F Minor Arpeggio

RH PLAY THE CHORD

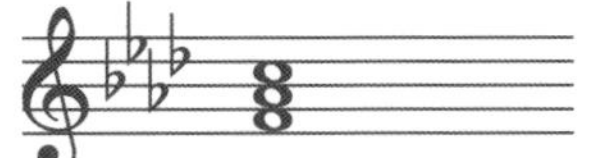

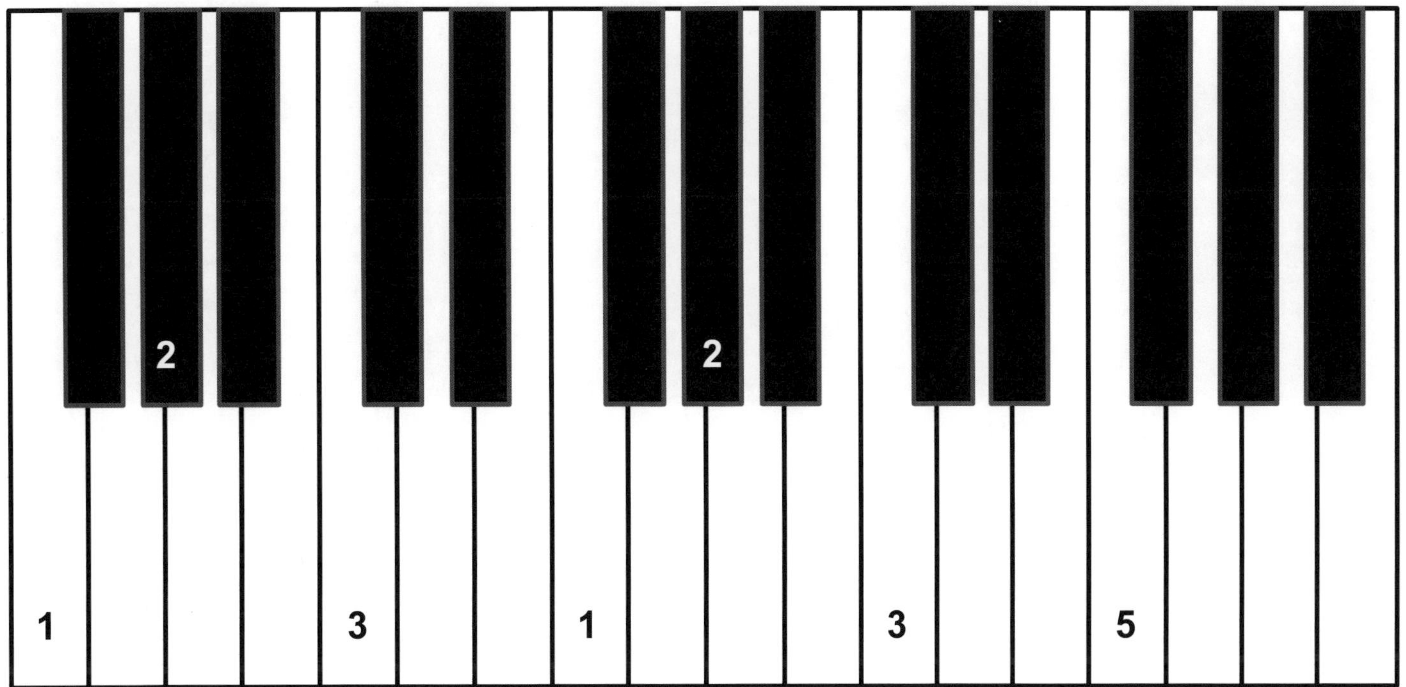

One black note

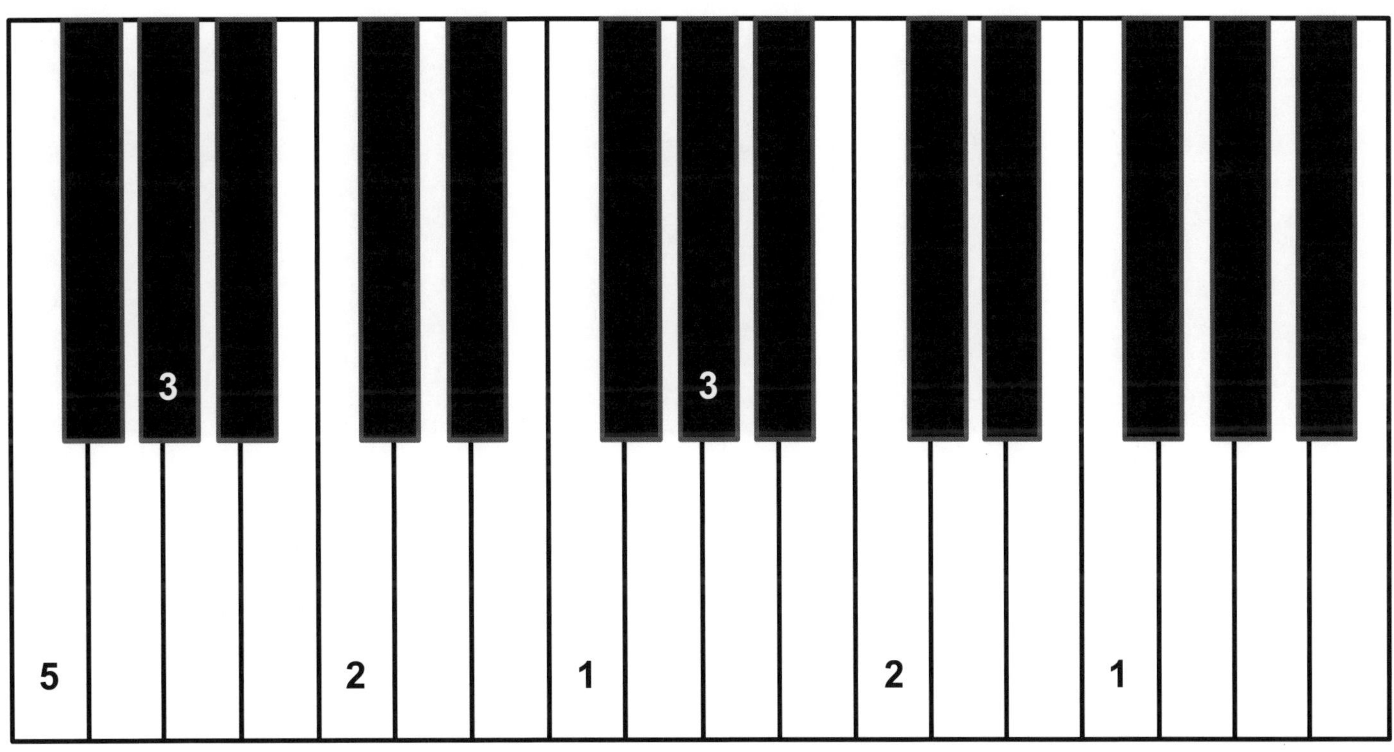

Group 1

F Minor Arpeggio

LH PLAY THE CHORD

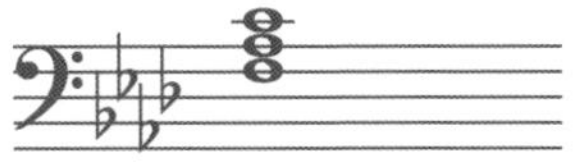

Group 1
B Major Arpeggio
RH PLAY THE CHORD

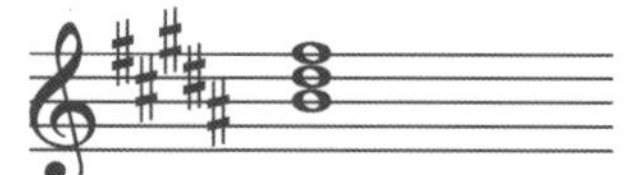

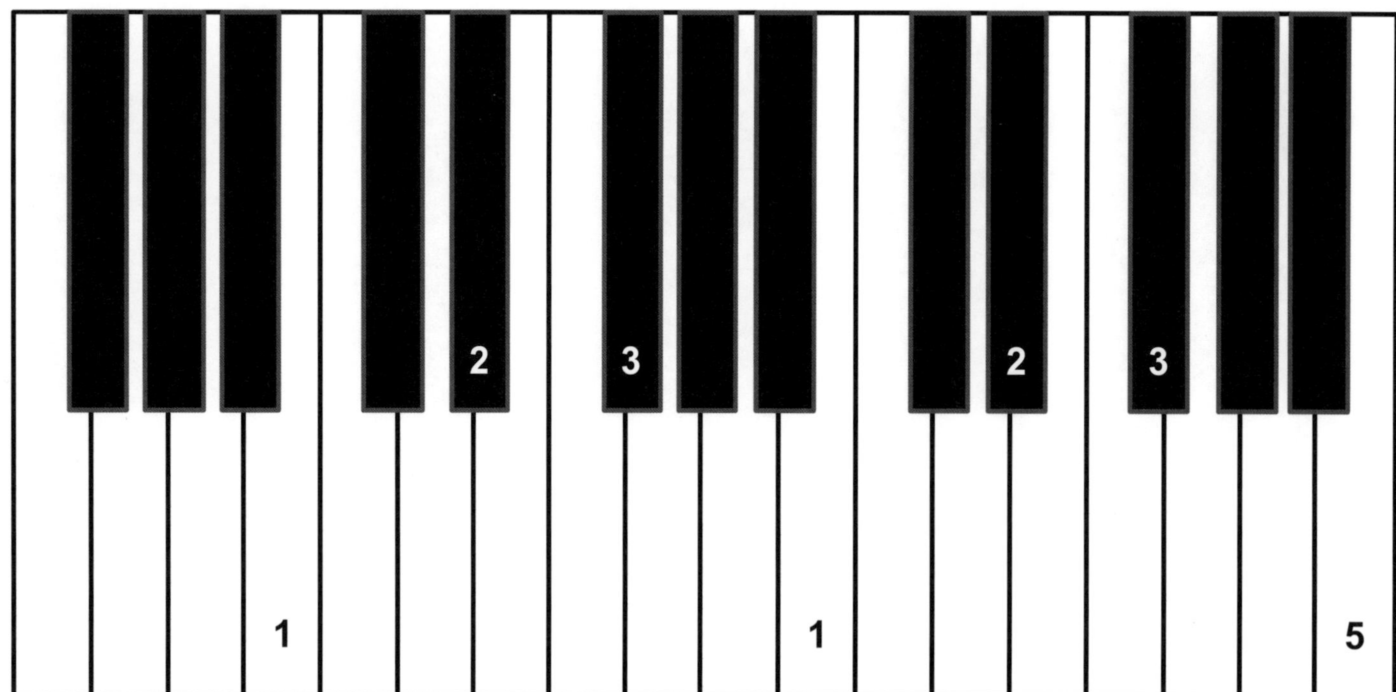

Two black notes

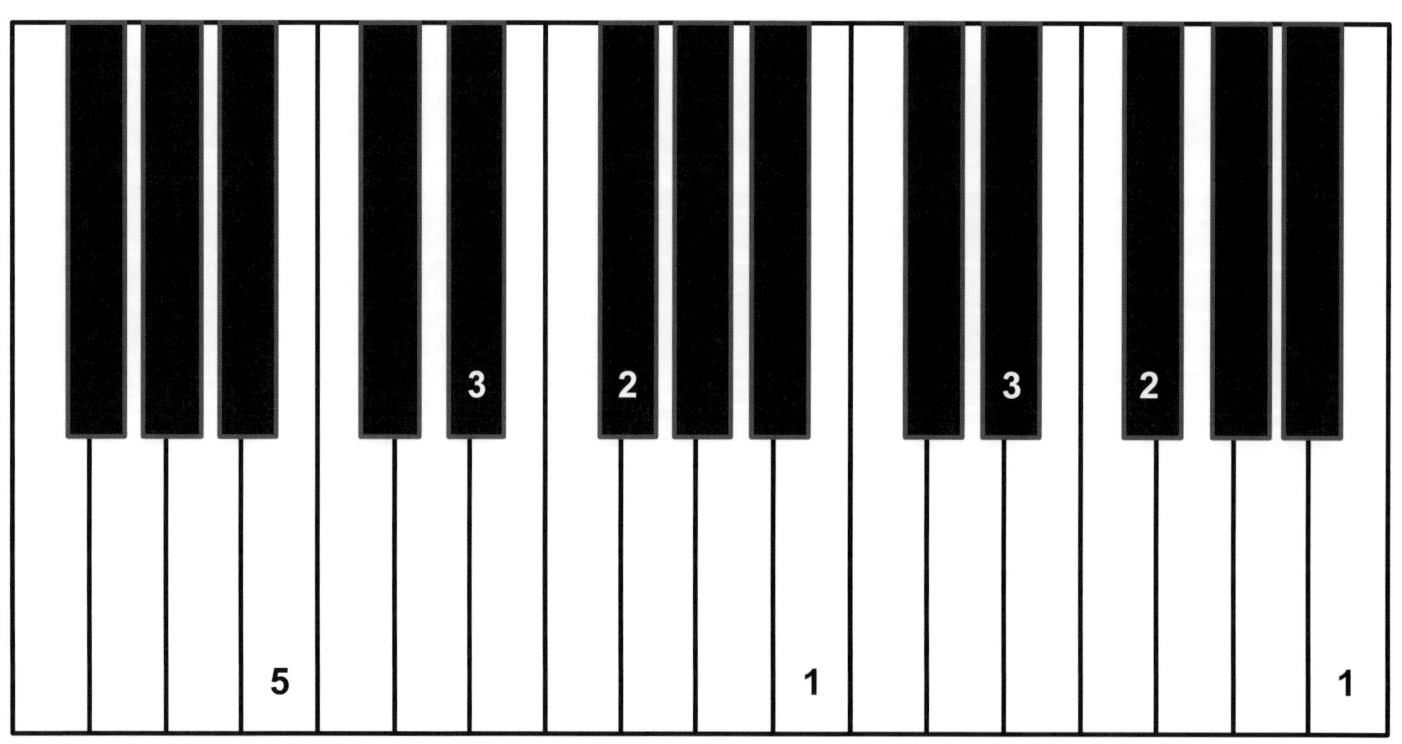

Group 1
B Major Arpeggio
LH PLAY THE CHORD

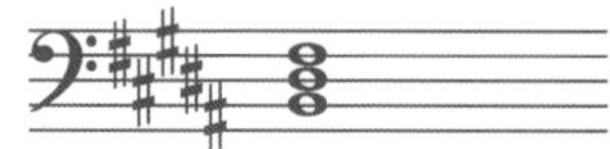

Group 1
B Minor Arpeggio
RH PLAY THE CHORD

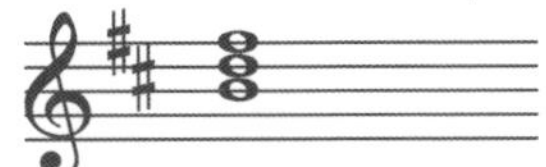

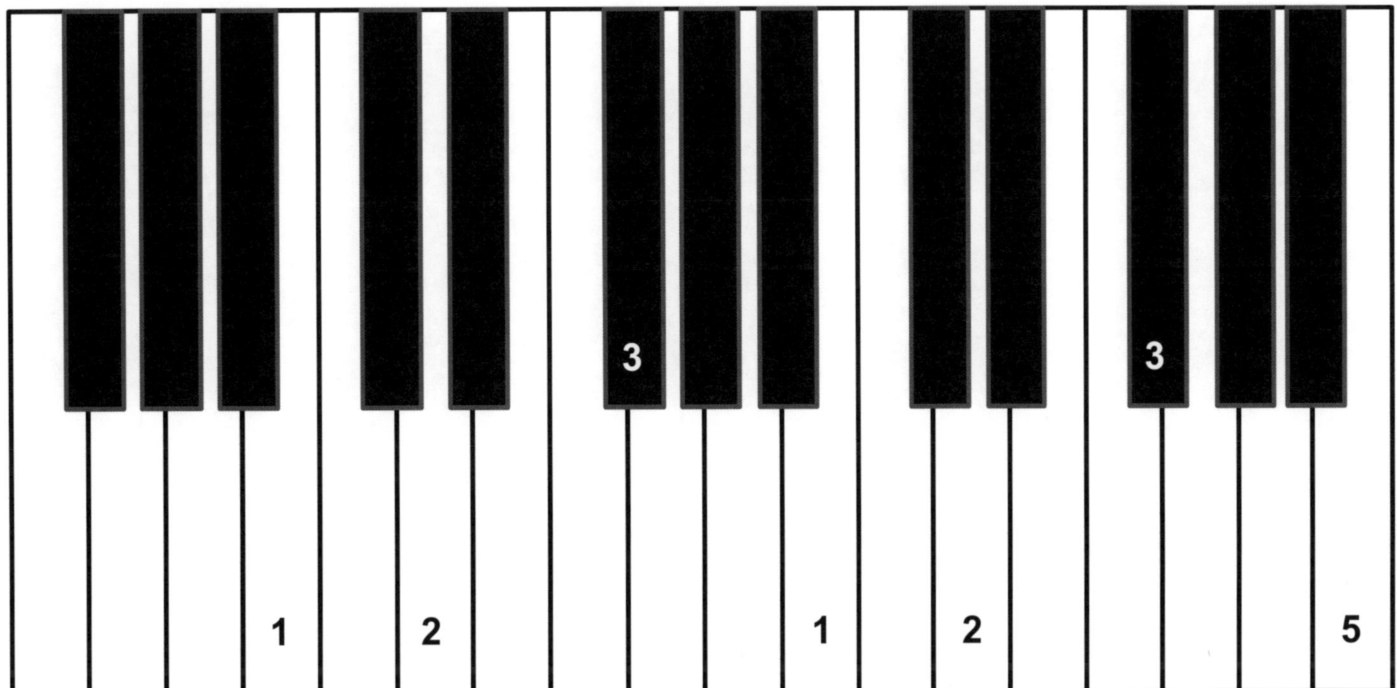

One black note

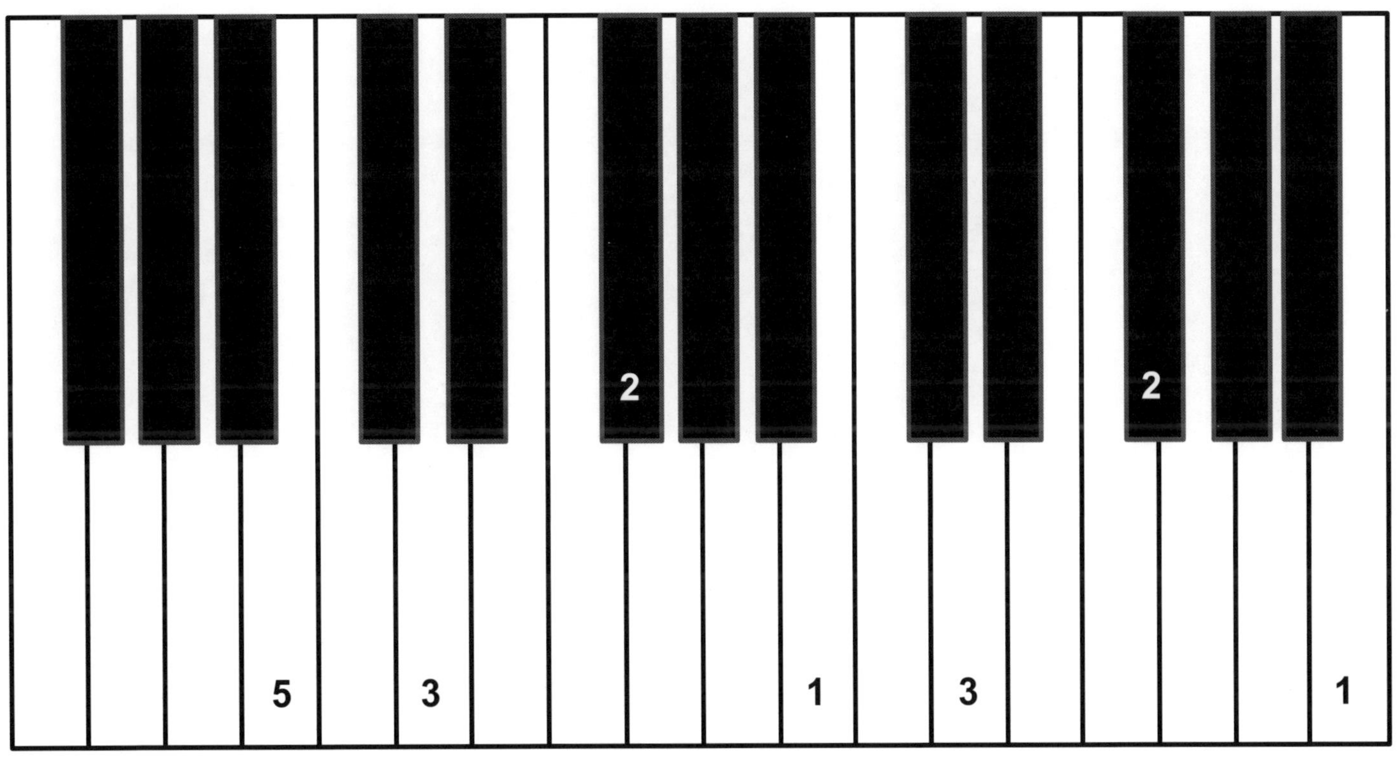

Group 1
B Minor Arpeggio
LH PLAY THE CHORD

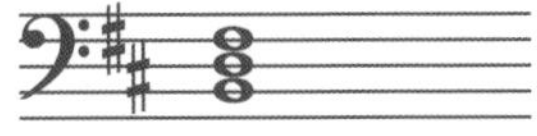

Group 1

F# Major Arpeggio

RH PLAY THE CHORD

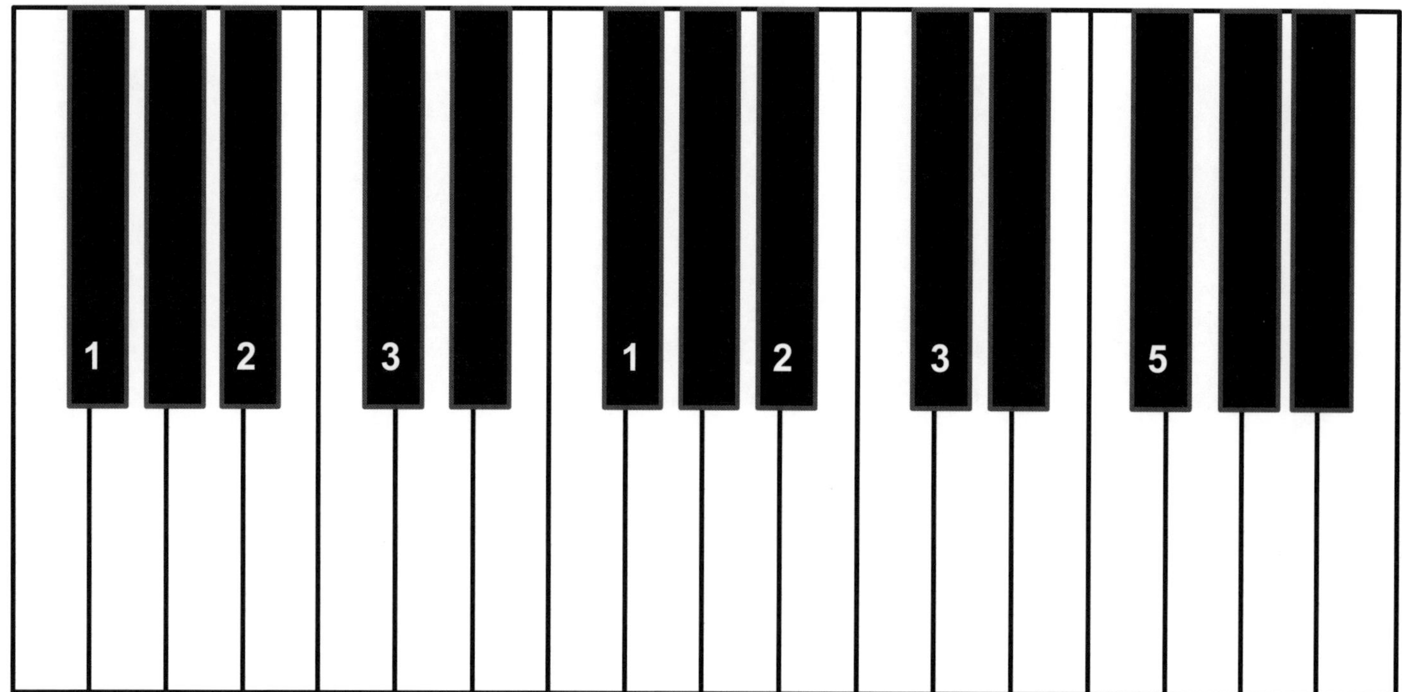

All black notes

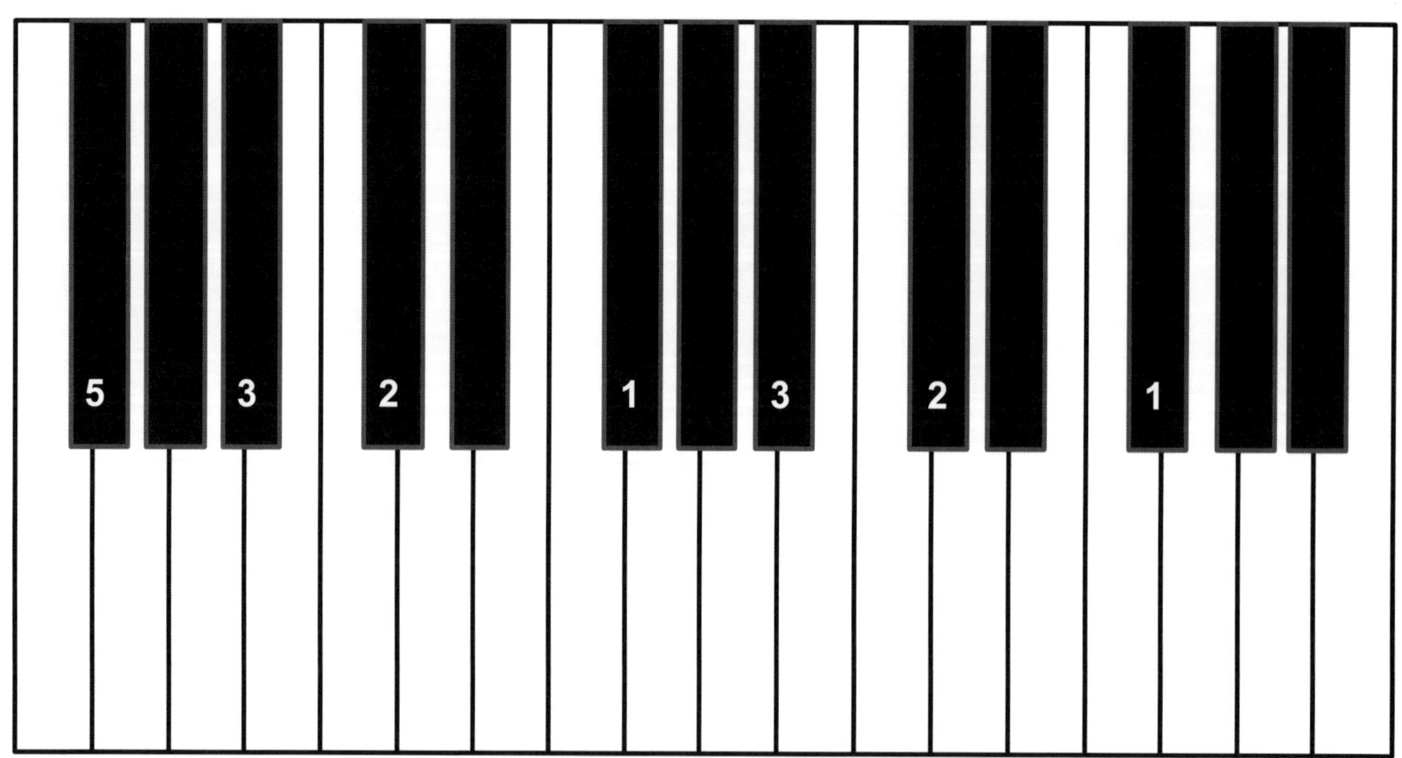

Group 1

F# Major Arpeggio

LH PLAY THE CHORD

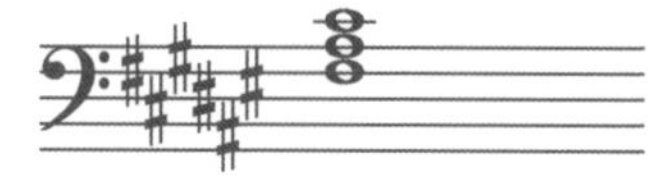

Group 1
Eb Minor Arpeggio
RH PLAY THE CHORD

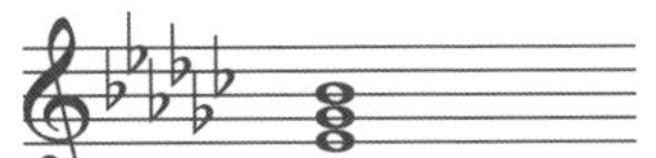

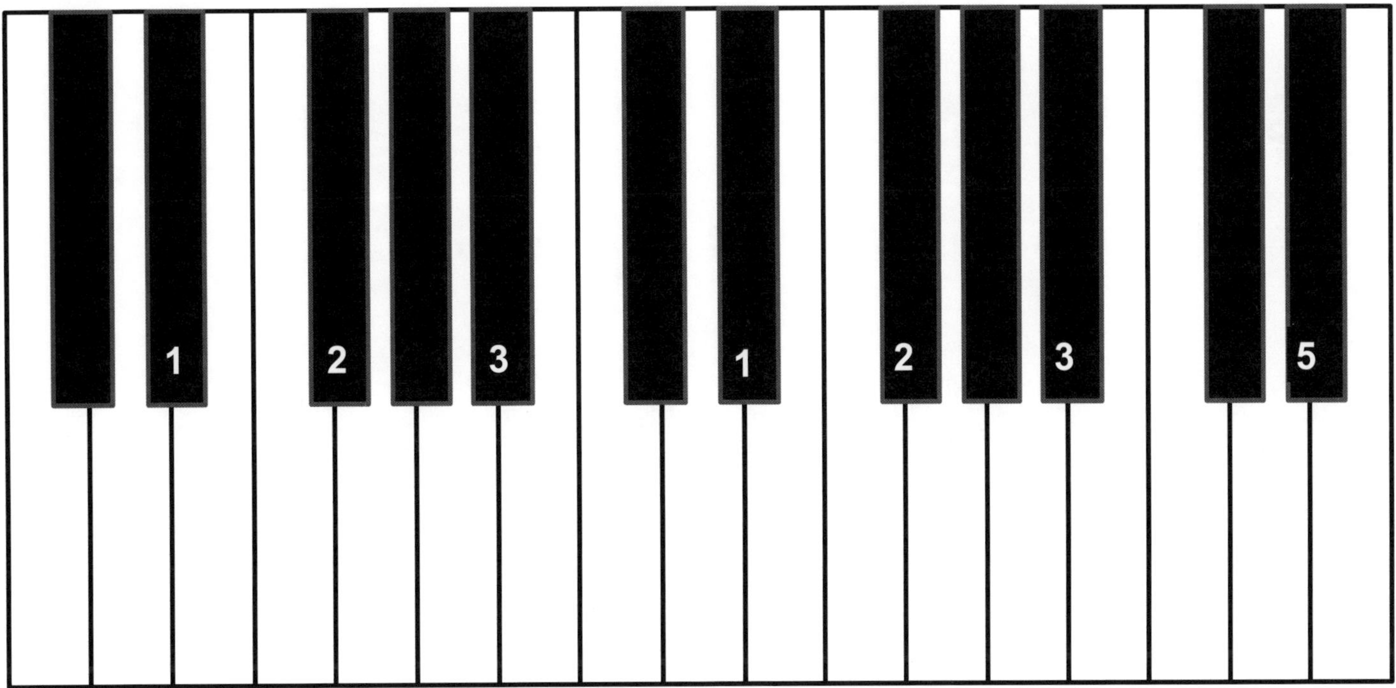

All black notes

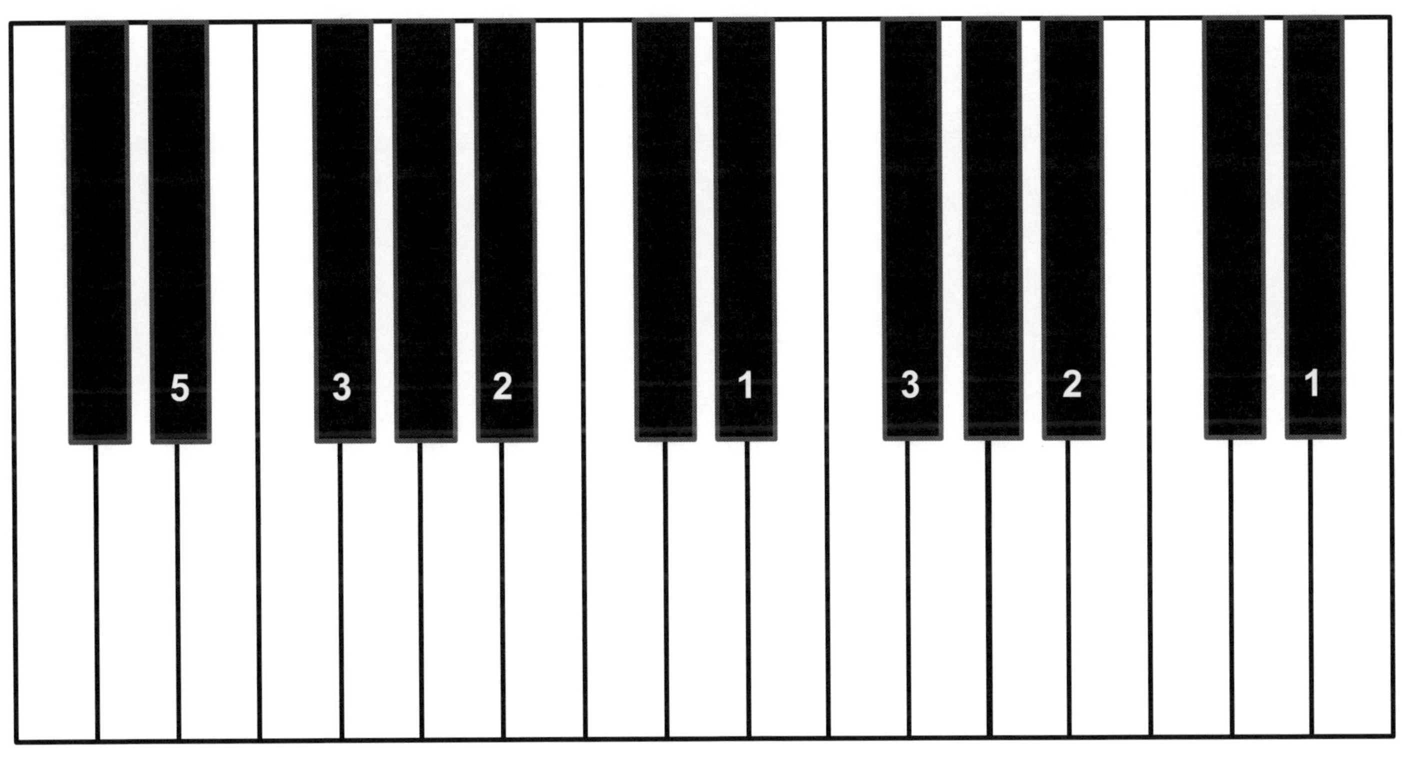

Group 1
Eb Minor Arpeggio
LH PLAY THE CHORD

Arpeggios

Group 2

Rule: No 3rd fingers

Eb major	G# minor	C# minor
Ab major	Db major	F# minor

Group 2
Eb Major Arpeggio
RH PLAY THE CHORD

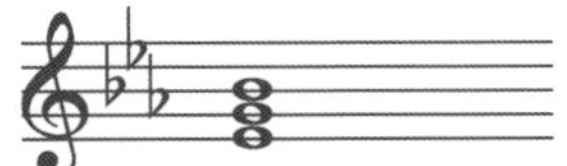

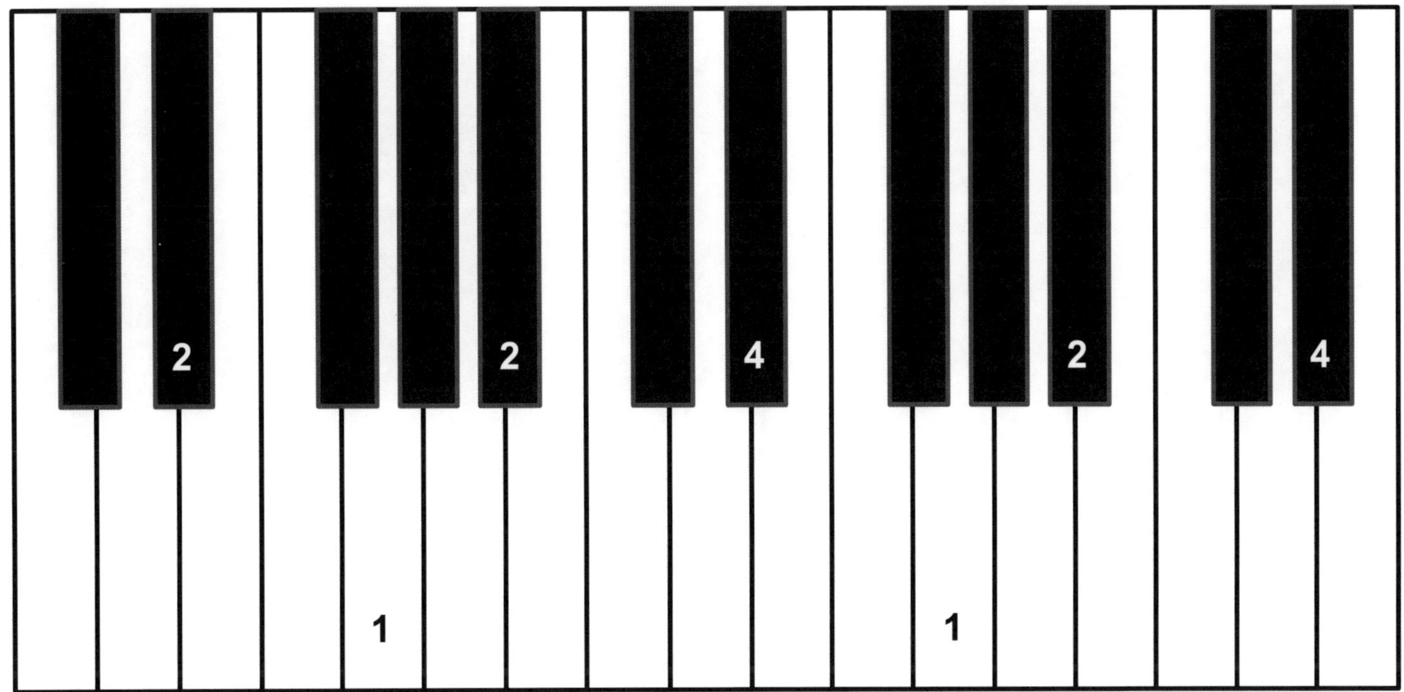

Fingers 2 and 4 on black notes

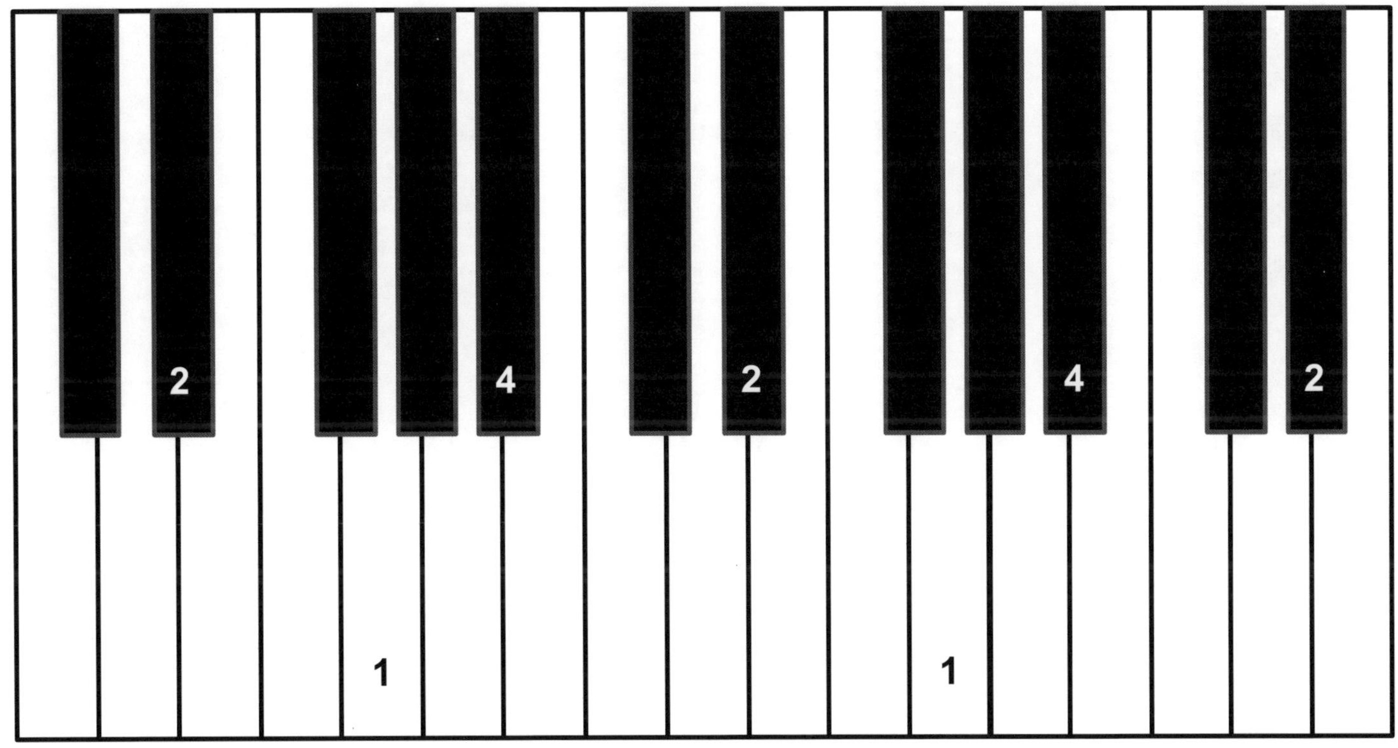

Group 2
Eb Major Arpeggio
LH PLAY THE CHORD

Group 2

Ab Major Arpeggio

RH PLAY THE CHORD

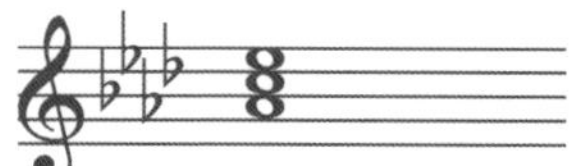

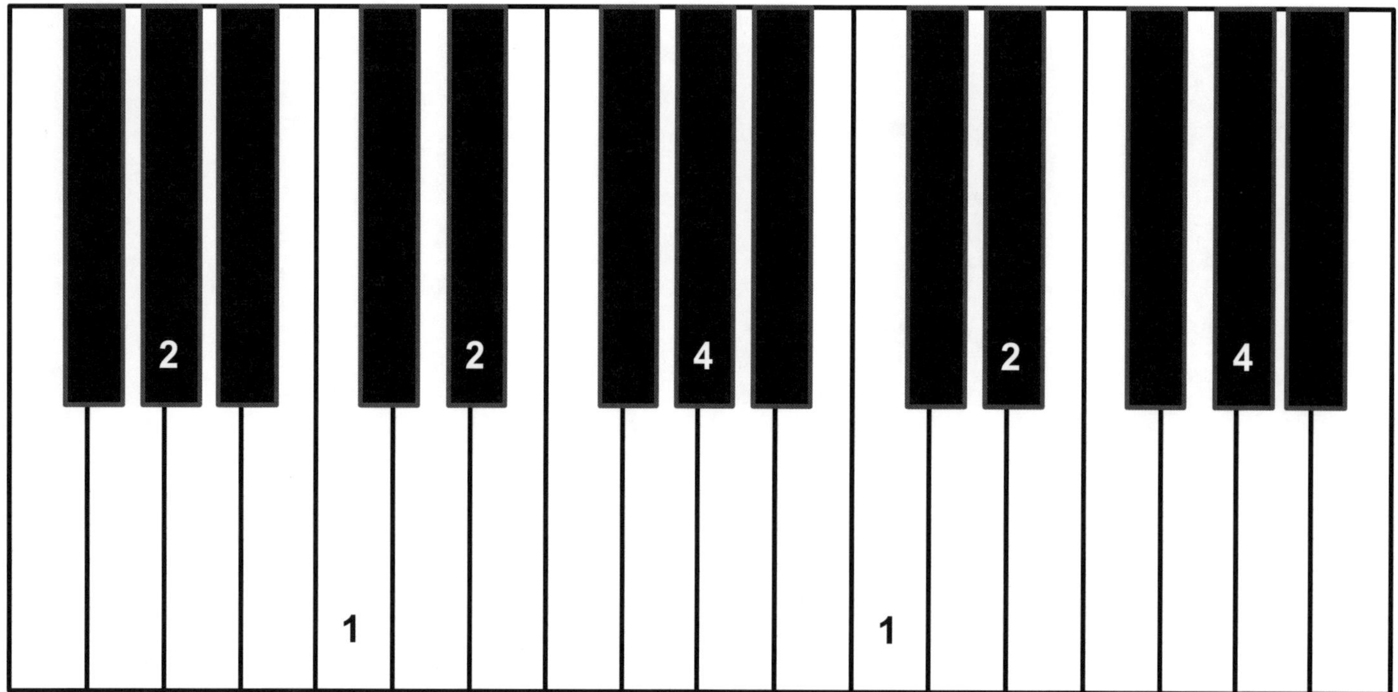

Fingers 2 and 4 on black notes

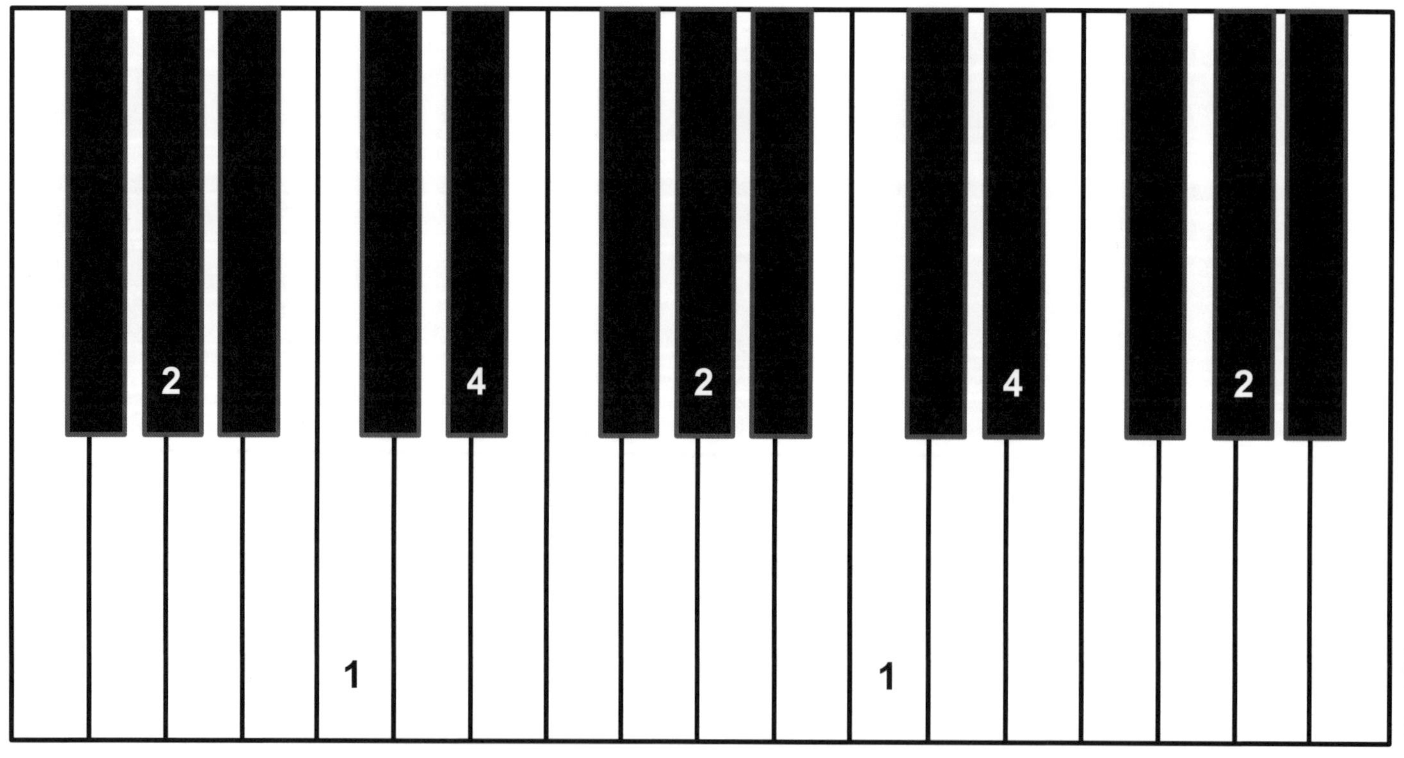

Group 2

Ab Major Arpeggio

LH PLAY THE CHORD

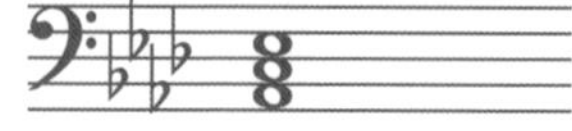

Group 2

G# Minor Arpeggio

RH PLAY THE CHORD

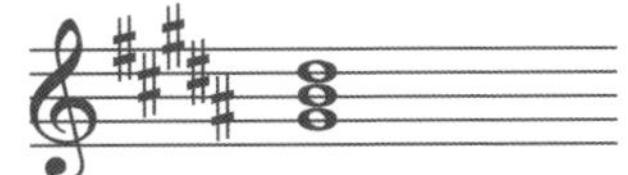

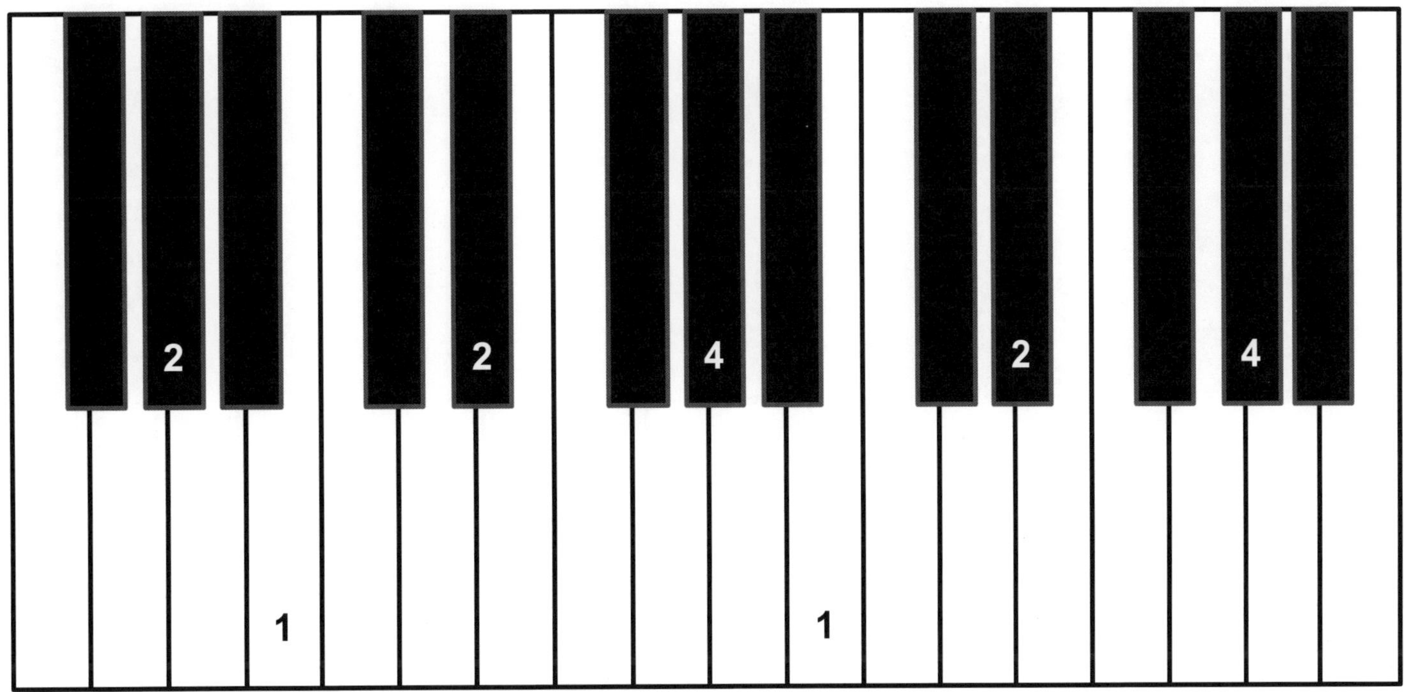

Fingers 2 and 4 on black notes

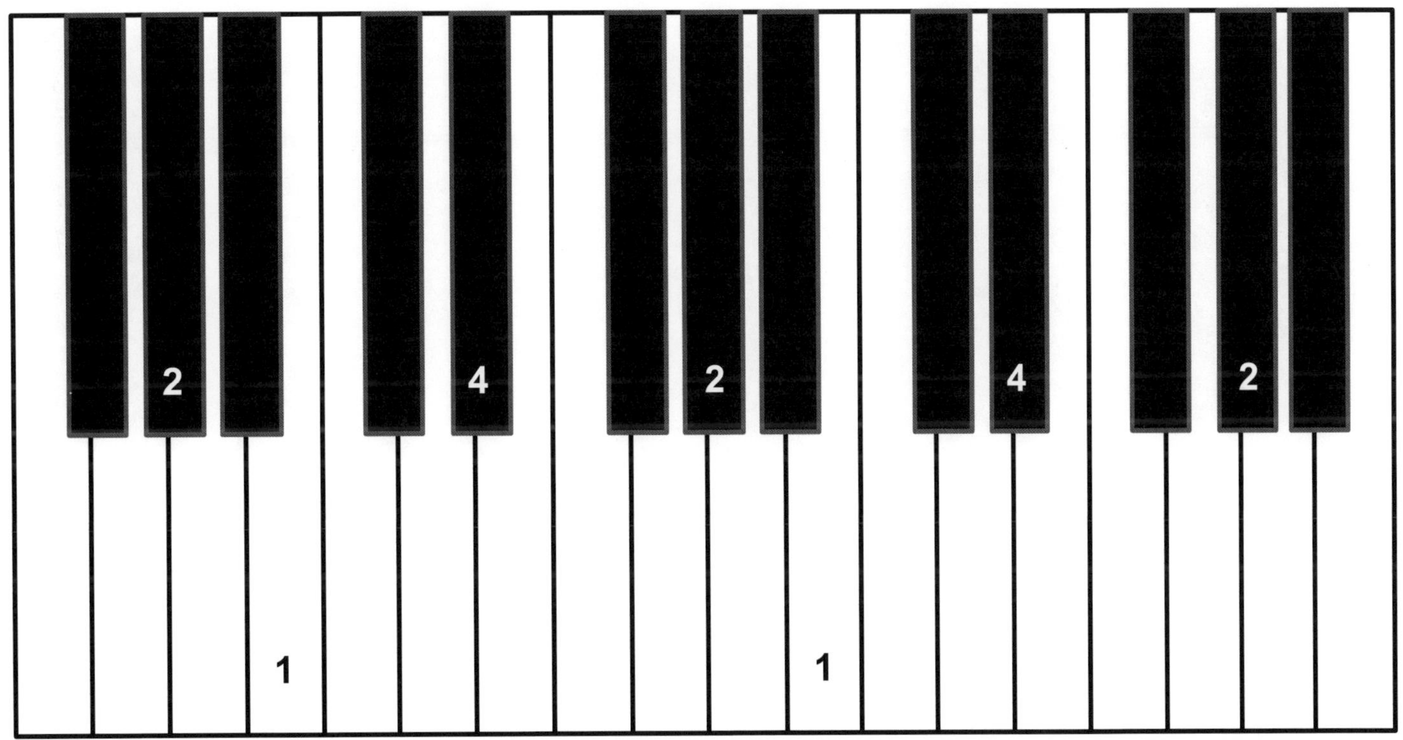

Group 2

G# Minor Arpeggio

LH PLAY THE CHORD

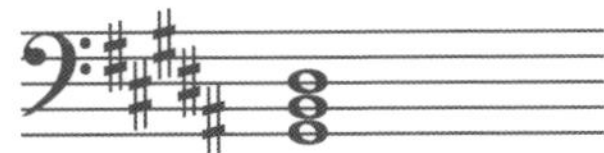

Group 2
Db Major Arpeggio
RH PLAY THE CHORD

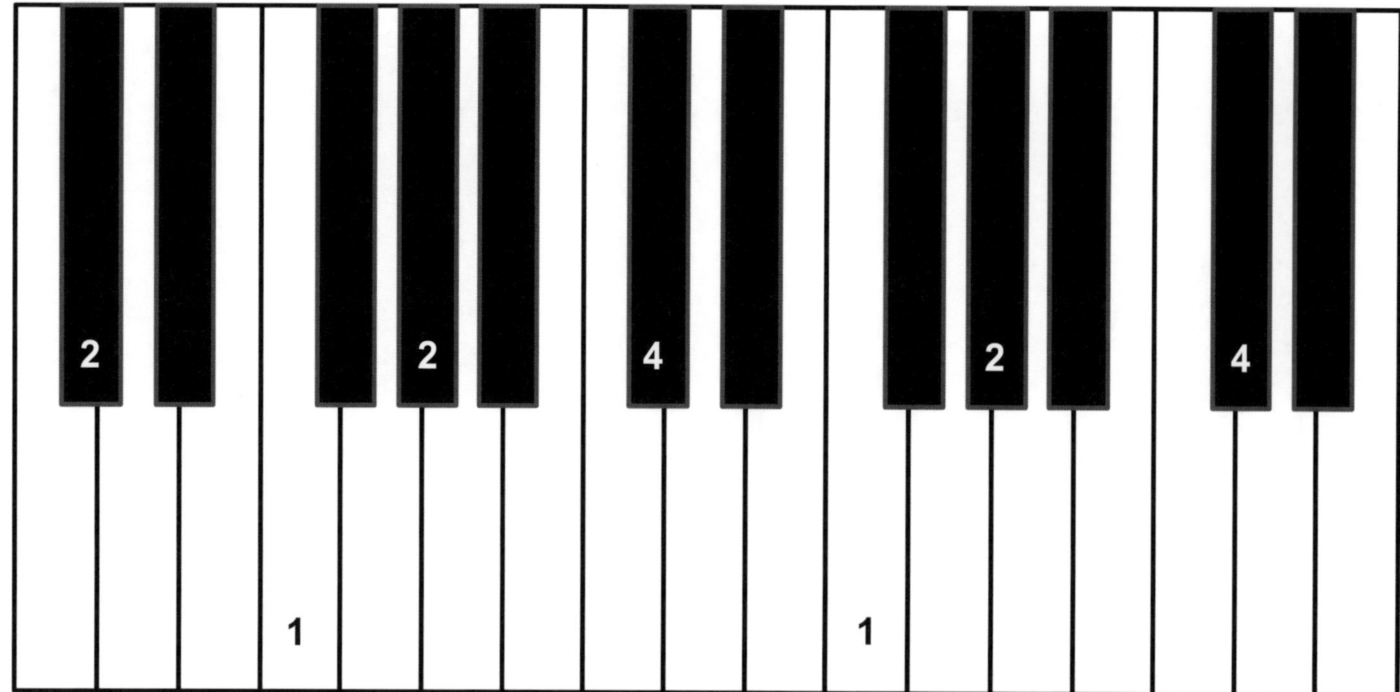

Fingers 2 and 4 on black notes

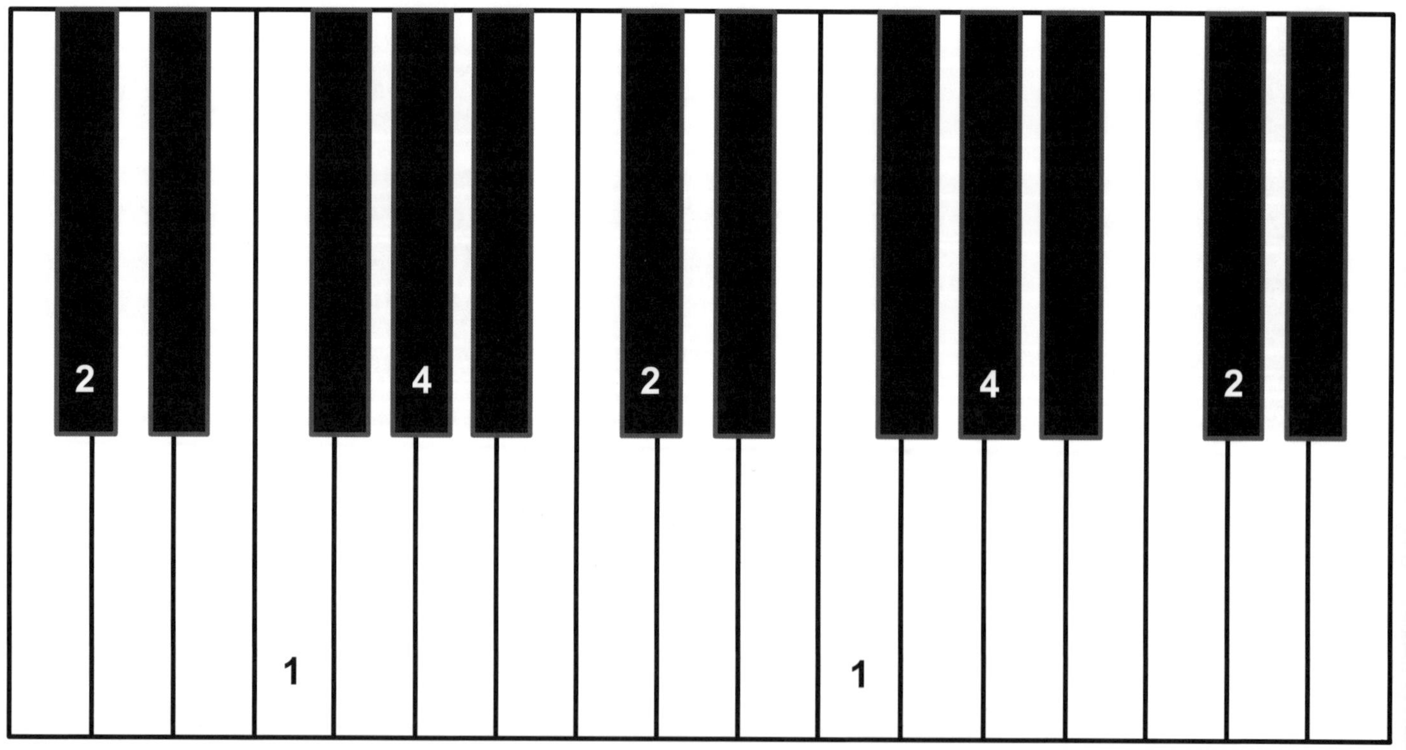

Group 2
Db Major Arpeggio
LH PLAY THE CHORD

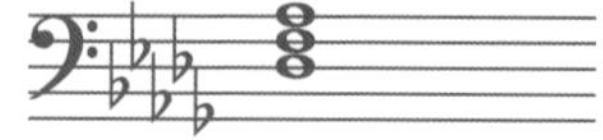

Group 2
C# Minor Arpeggio
RH PLAY THE CHORD

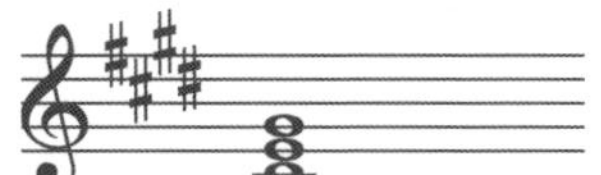

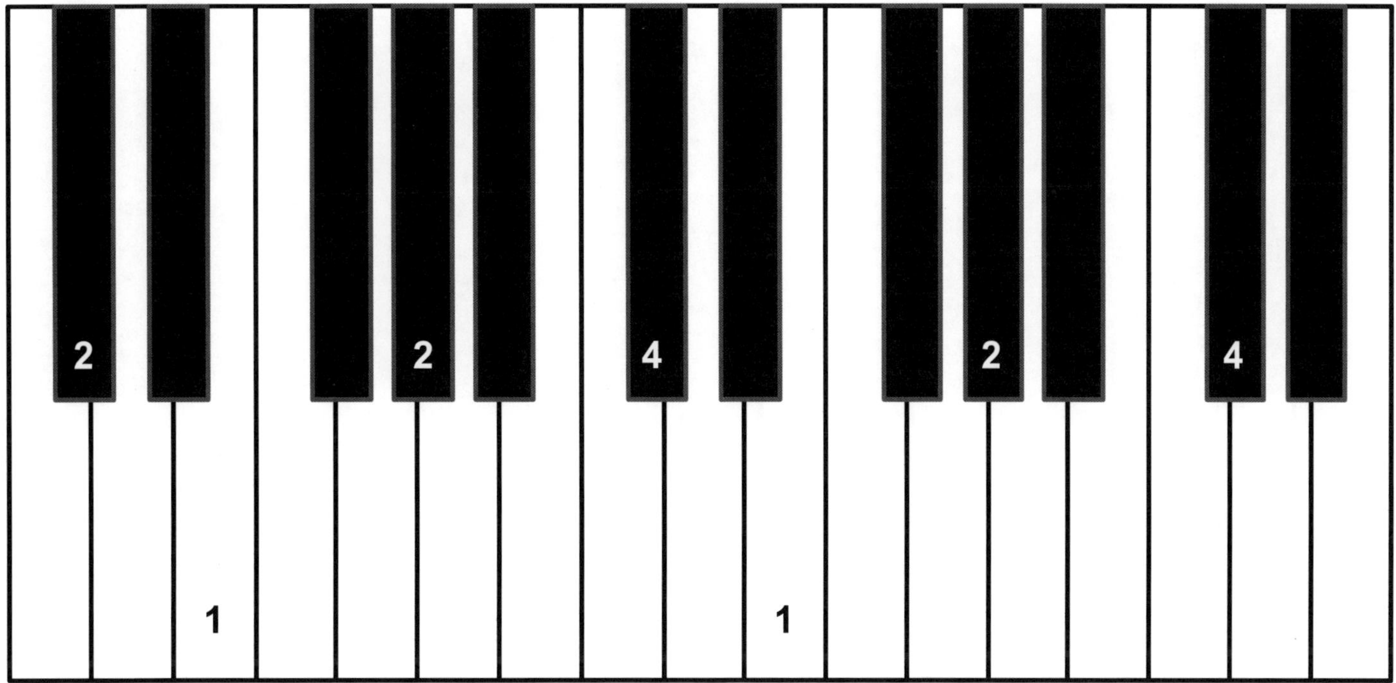

Fingers 2 and 4 on black notes

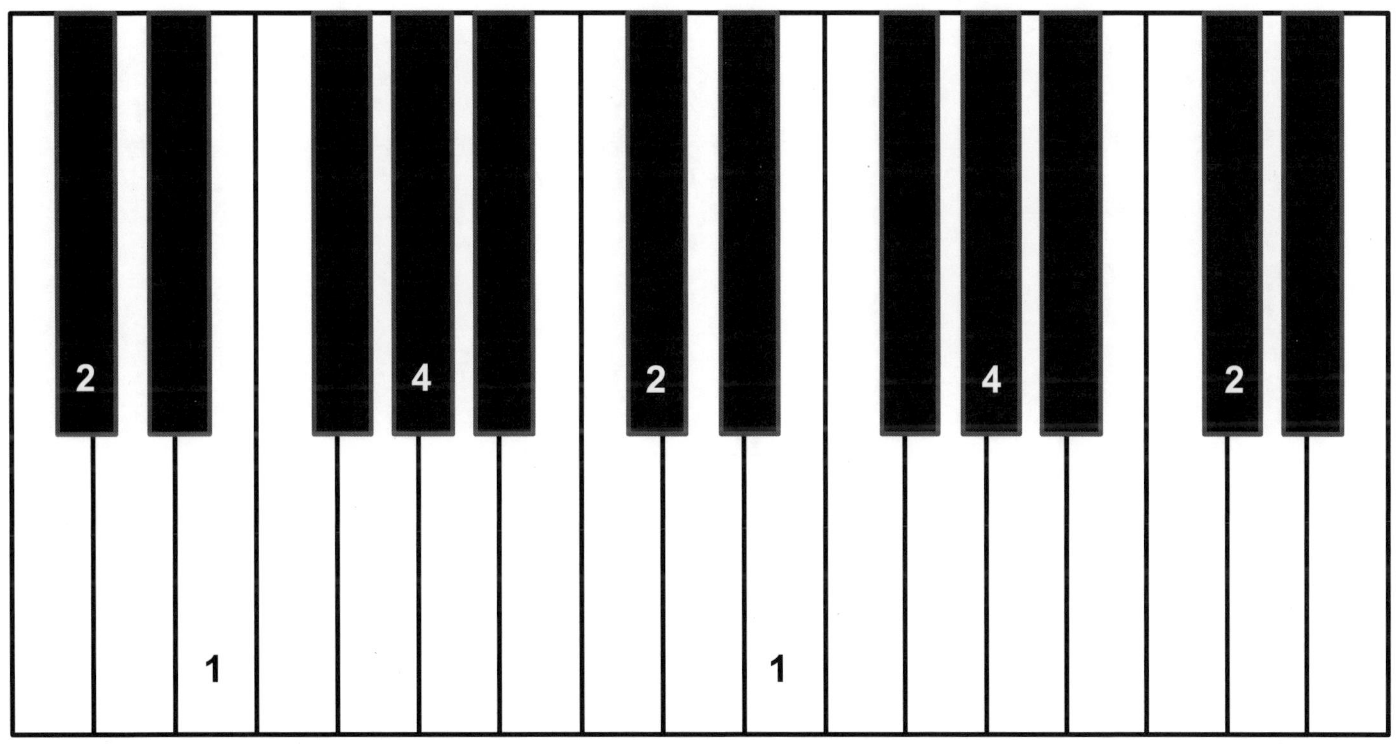

Group 2
C# Minor Arpeggio
LH PLAY THE CHORD

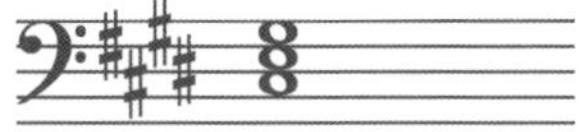

Group 2
F# Minor Arpeggio
RH PLAY THE CHORD

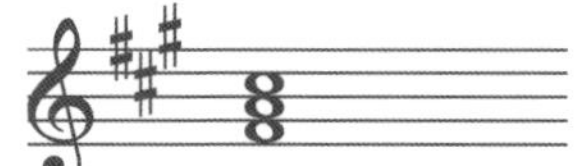

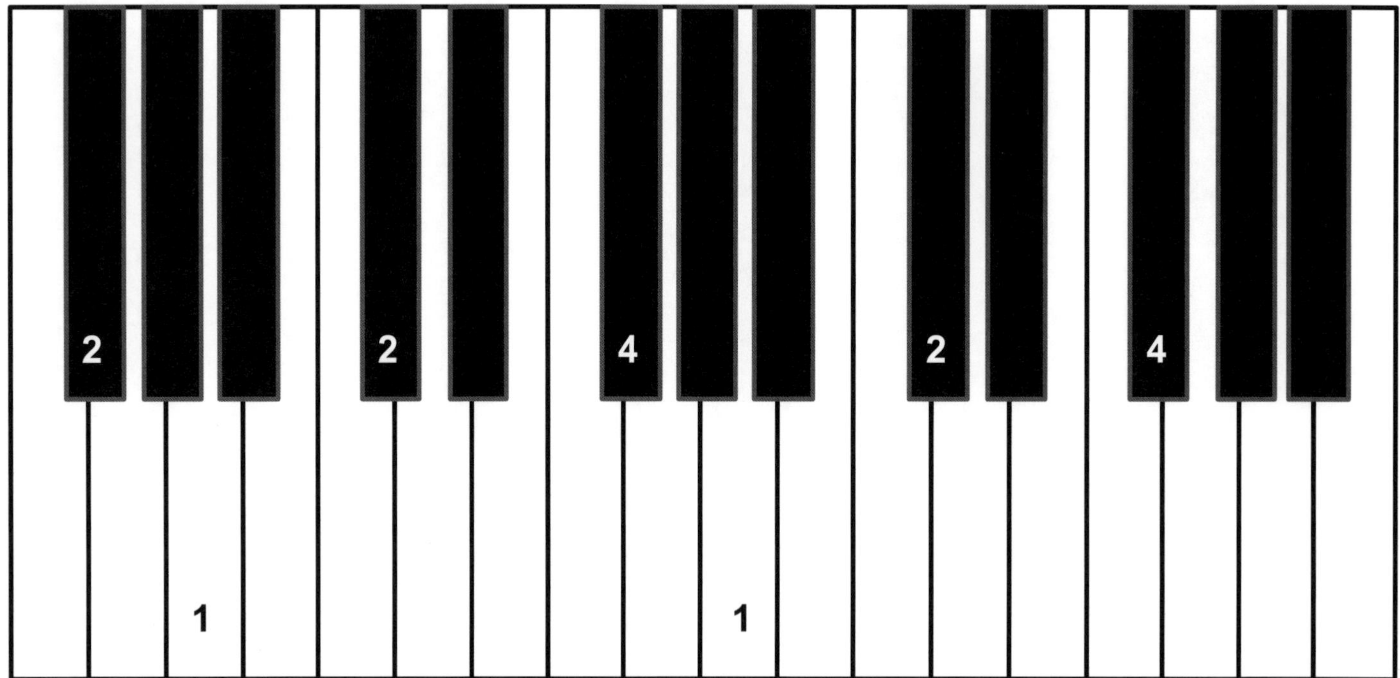

Fingers 2 and 4 on black notes

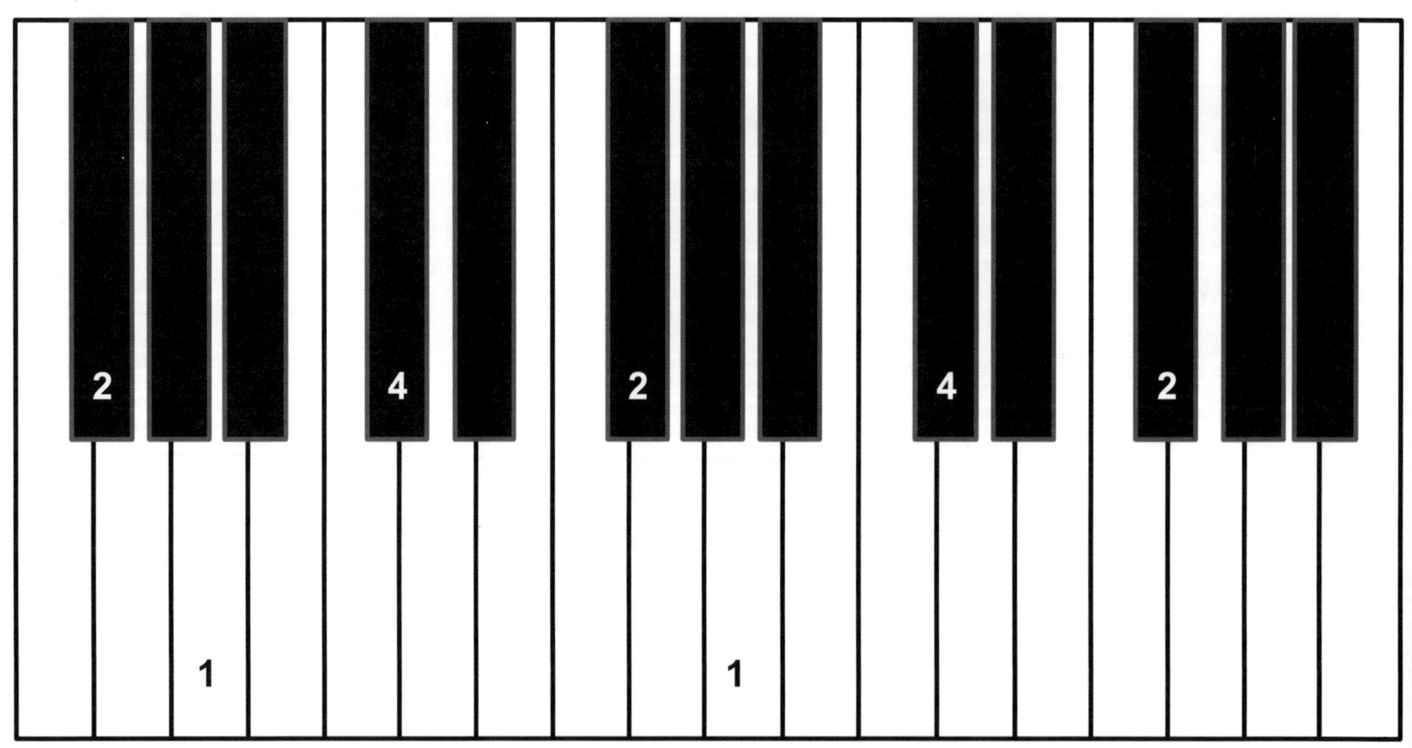

Group 2
F# Minor Arpeggio
LH PLAY THE CHORD

Arpeggios

Group 3

Check individual fingering for these

Bb major   Bb minor

Group 3

Bb Major Arpeggio

RH PLAY THE CHORD

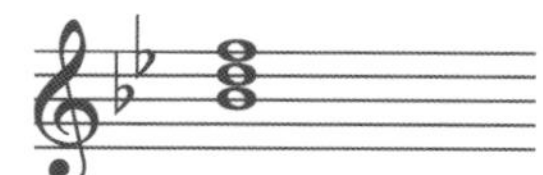

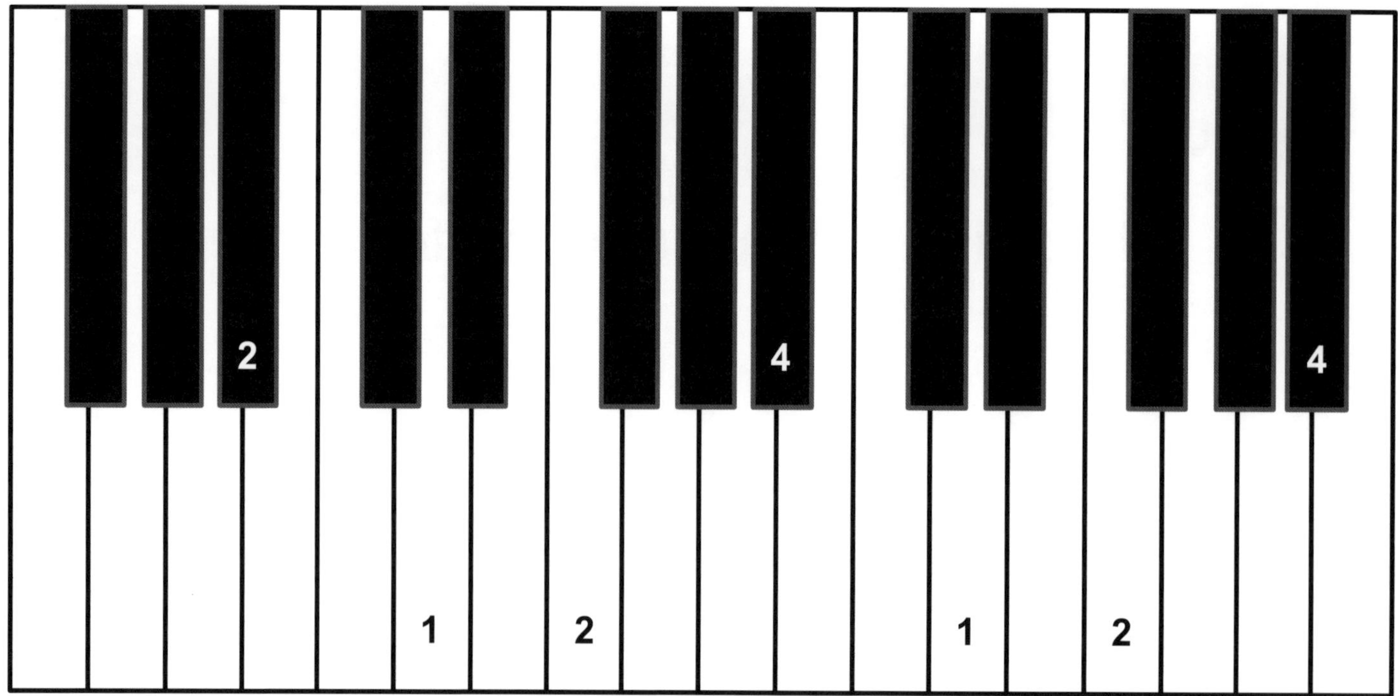

RH fingers 2 and 4 on black notes
LH finger 3 on Bb

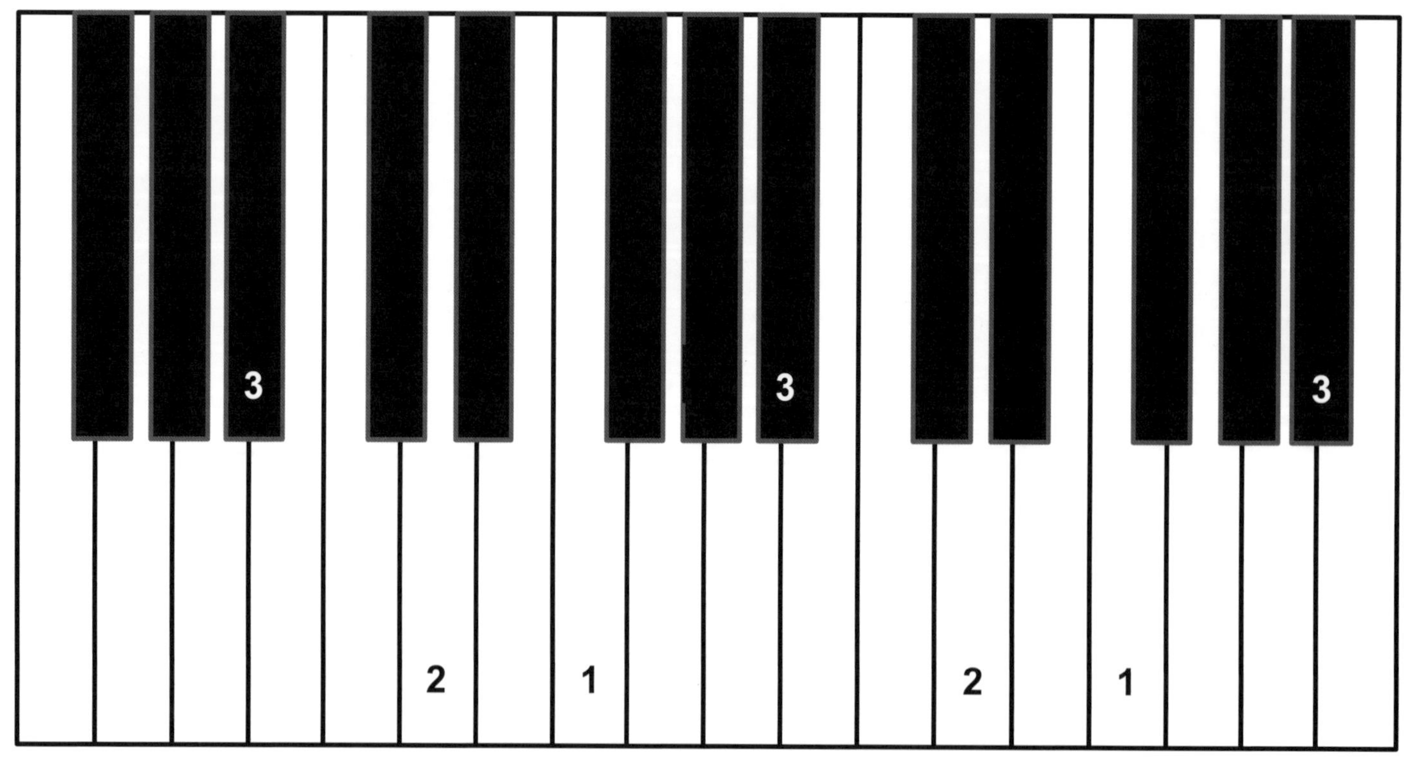

Group 3

Bb Major Arpeggio

LH PLAY THE CHORD

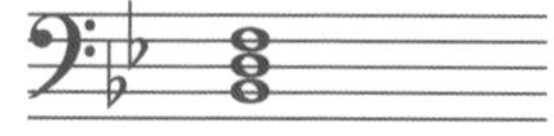

Group 3
Bb Minor Arpeggio
RH PLAY THE CHORD

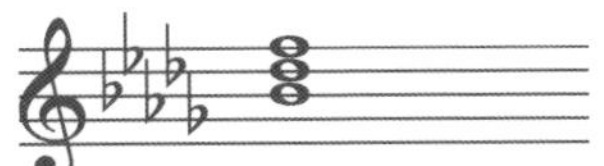

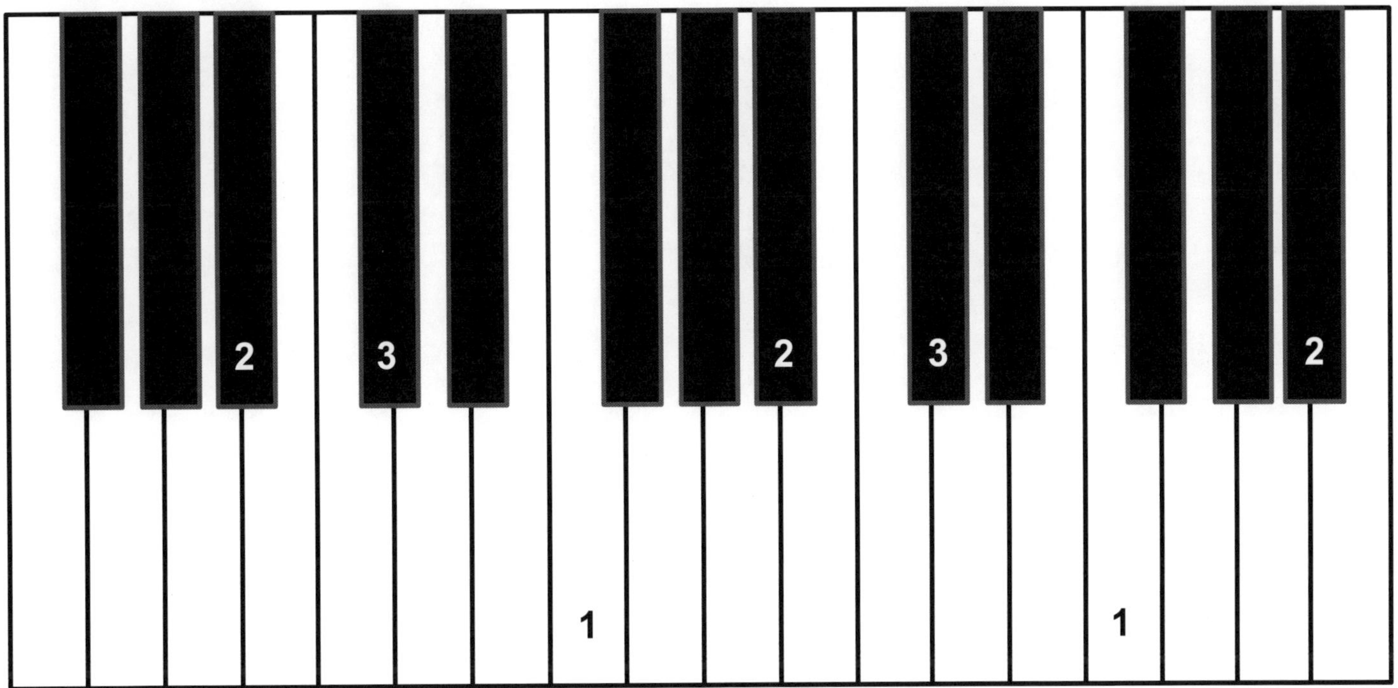

Fingers 2 and 3 on black notes

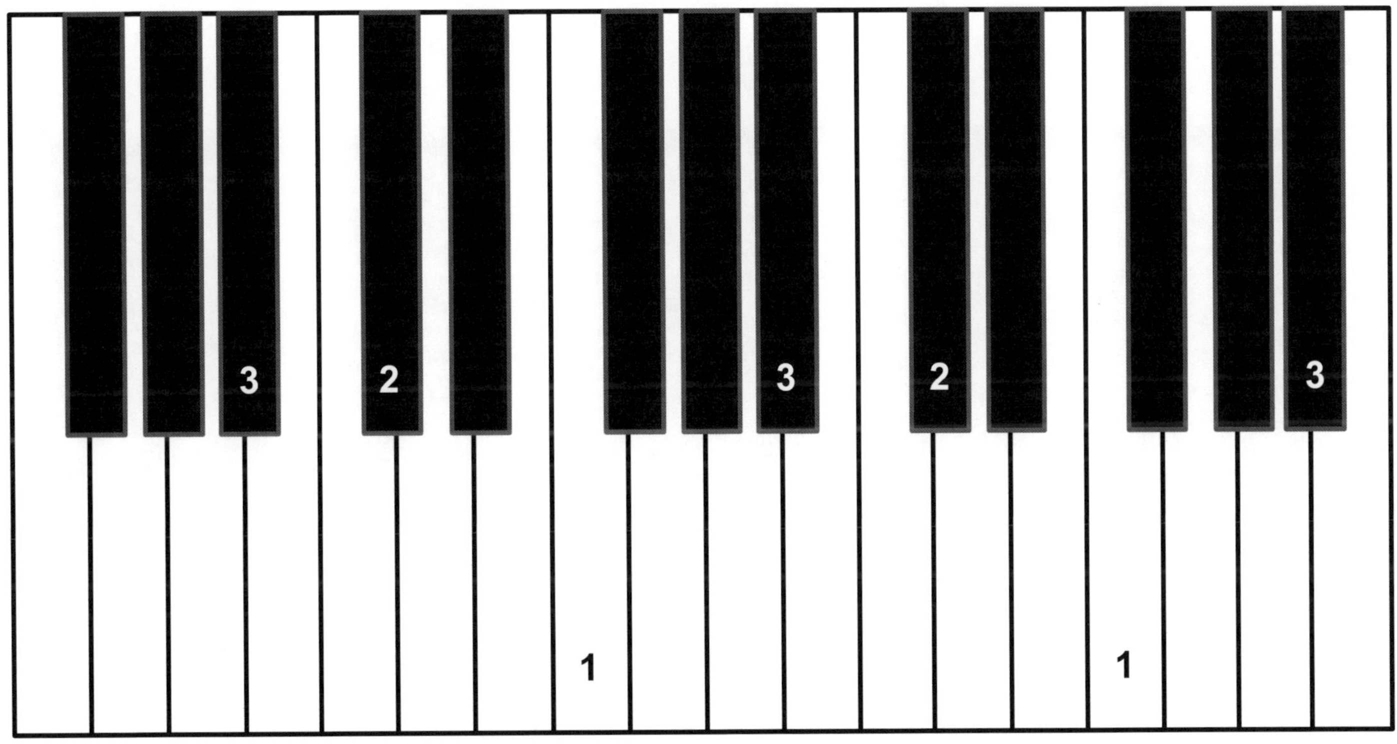

Group 3
Bb Minor Arpeggio
LH PLAY THE CHORD

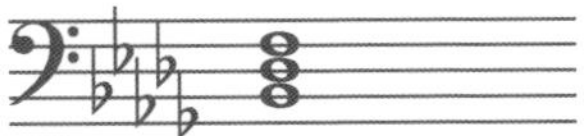

Chromatic Scale starting on A
RH

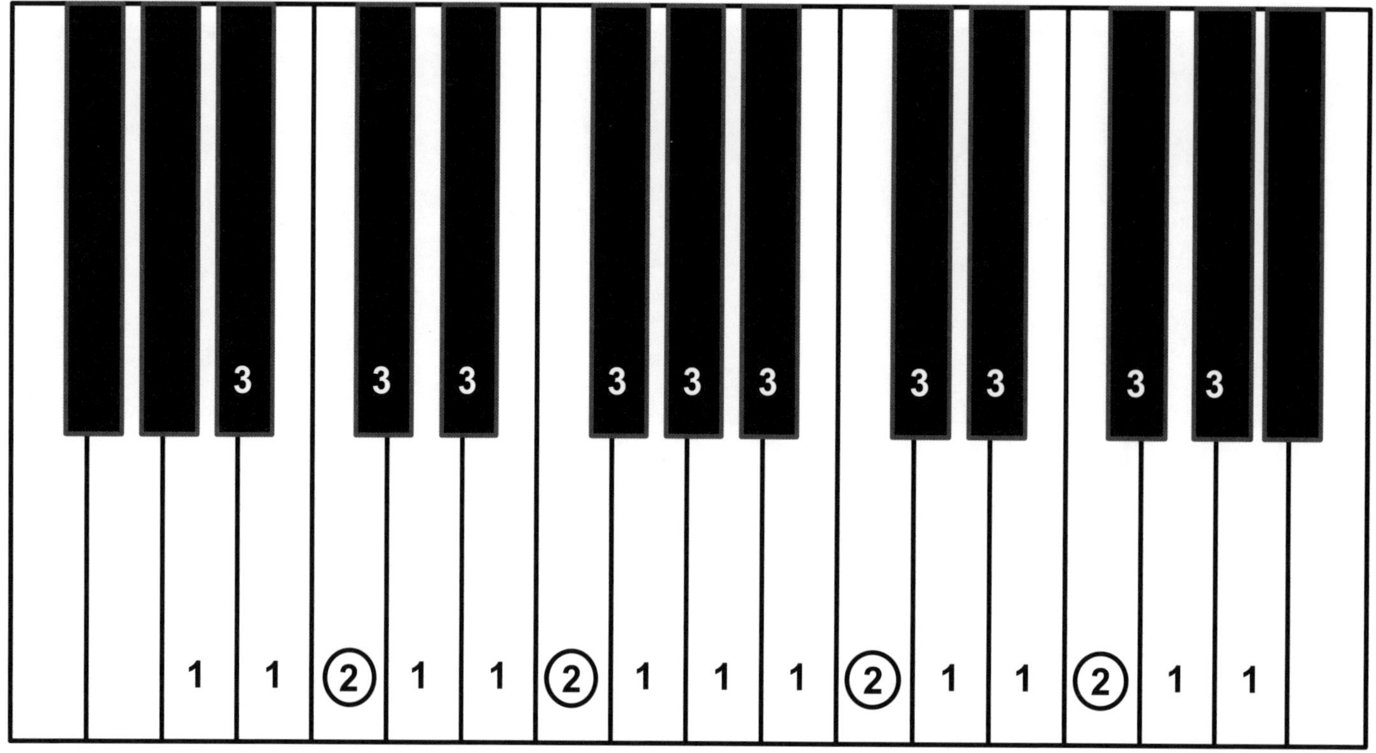

Chromatic Scale starting on A
LH

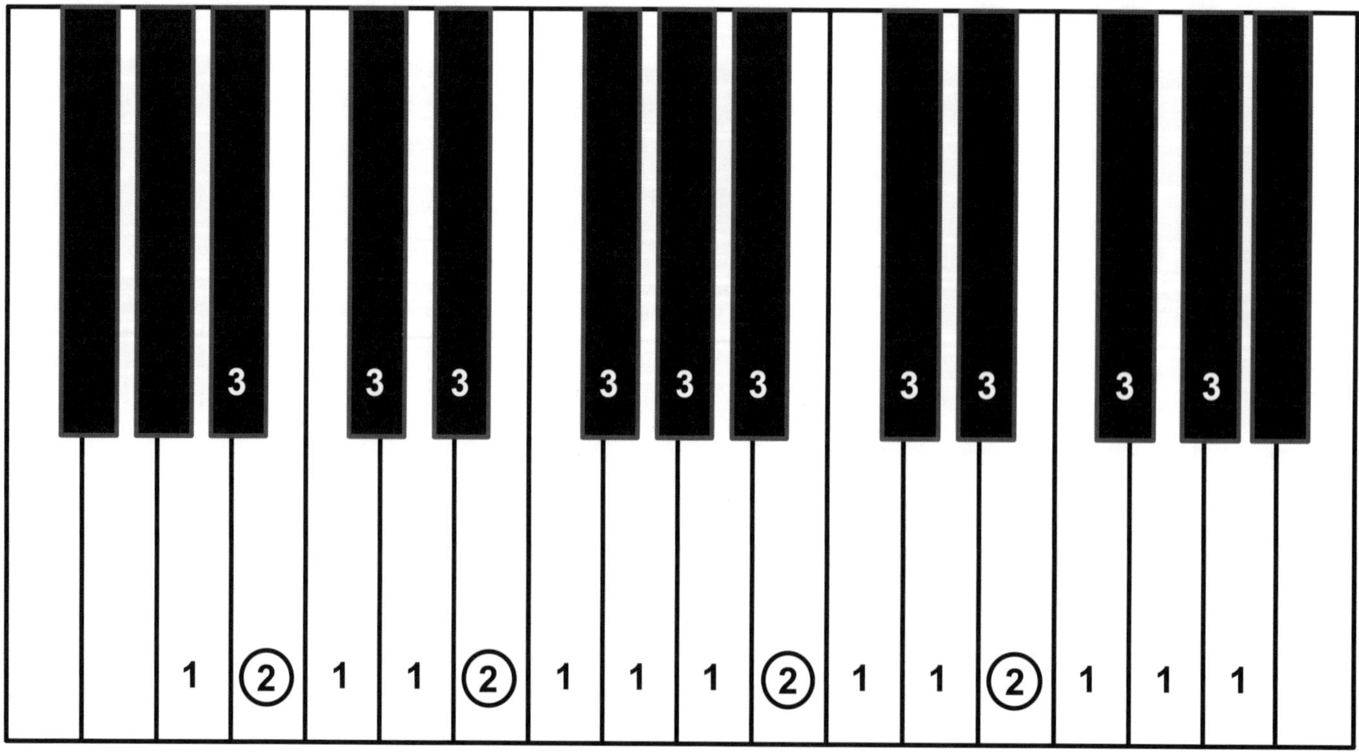

Contrary Motion Scales

- **Look at the diagram without playing**
- **Compare the fingering on the black notes with the fingering on the white notes**

The fingering is usually the same for both RH and LH.

For example:

C# minor

White notes in both hands, fingers 1 and 2 only

C minor

Black notes in both hands, 3rd fingers only

Tips for some contrary motion scales:

- **All minor contrary motion scales:** look at the keyboard and memorise the shape of the first four notes, hands together.

- **E major:** say, 'white, black black, white white, black black, white' etc. as you play.

- **Eb major:** 3rd fingers on Eb. Say, 'black, white white, black black, white white, black', etc. as you play.

C Major
Contrary Motion Scale
PLAY THE CHORD

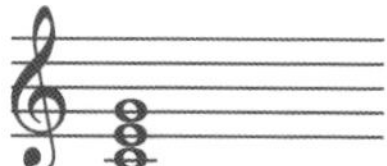

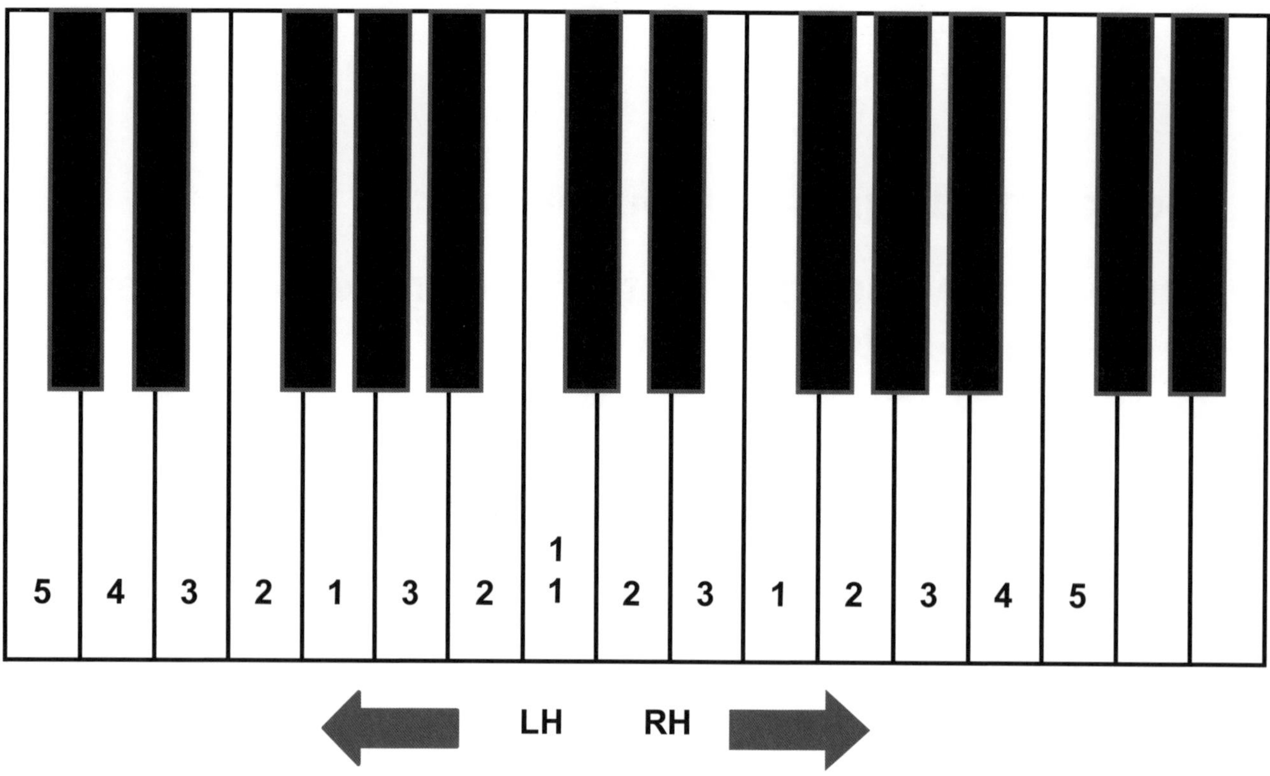

LH RH

E Major
Contrary Motion scale
PLAY THE CHORD

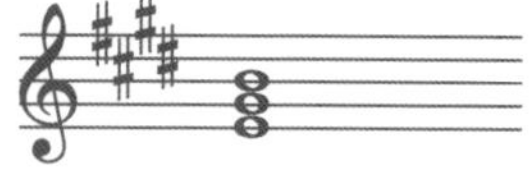

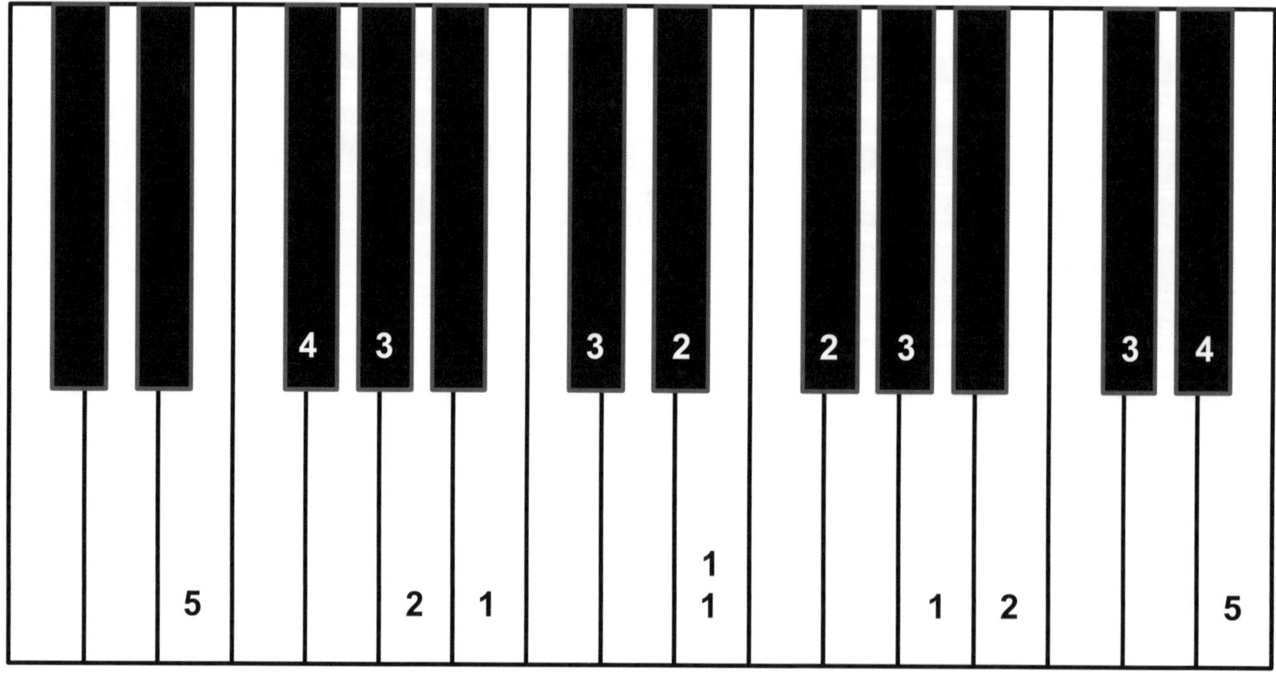

A Major
Contrary Motion Scale
PLAY THE CHORD

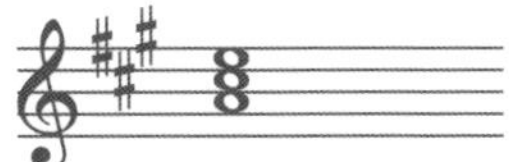

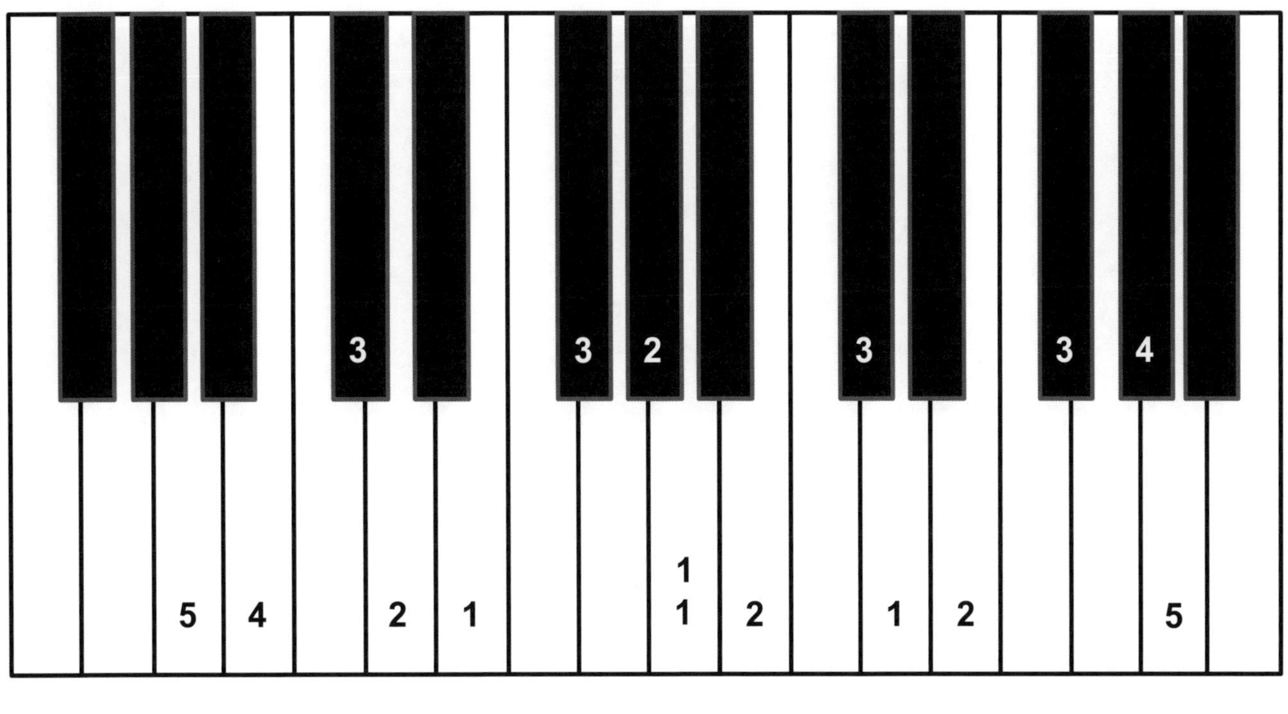

A Harmonic Minor
Contrary Motion Scale
PLAY THE CHORD

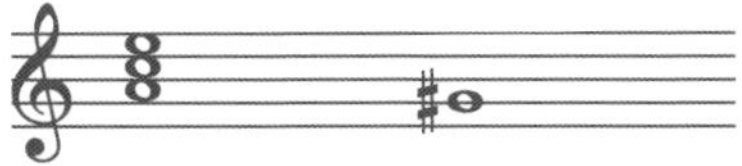

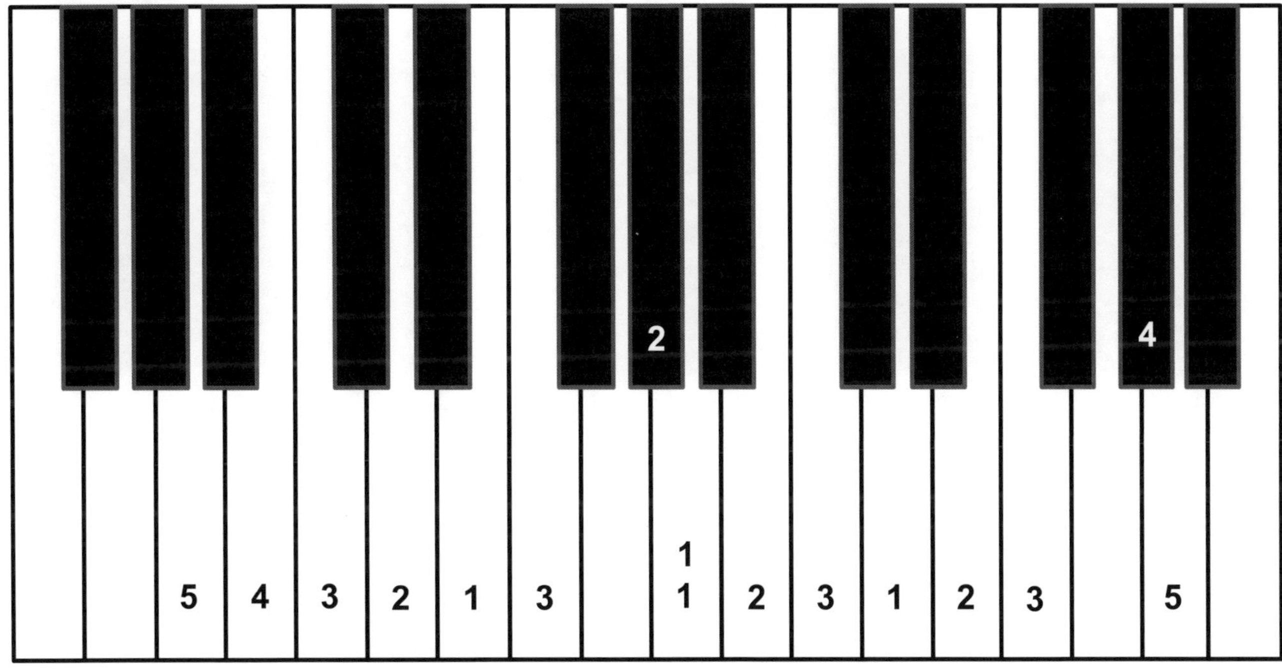

F Major
Contrary Motion Scale
PLAY THE CHORD

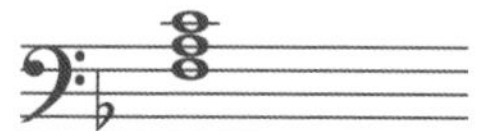

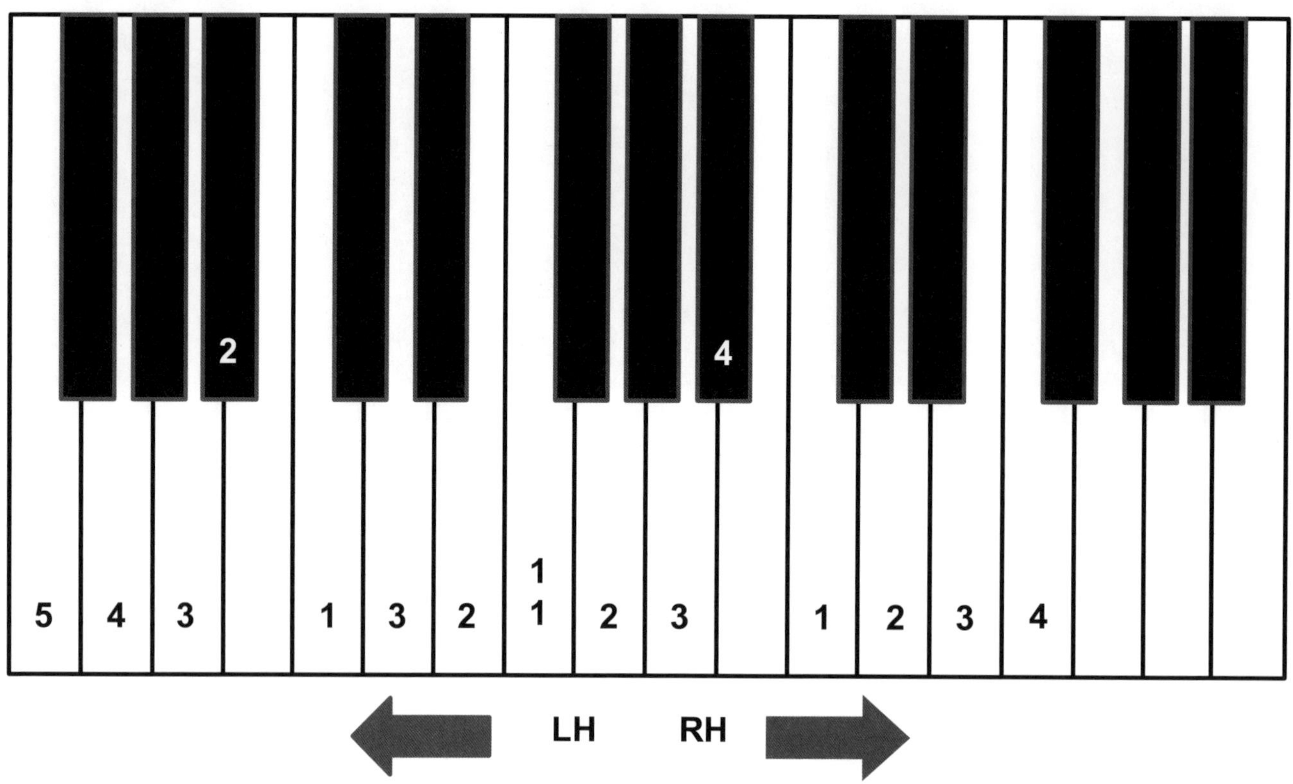

Eb Major
Contrary Motion Scale
PLAY THE CHORD

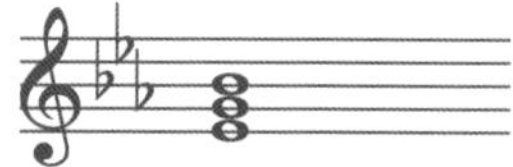

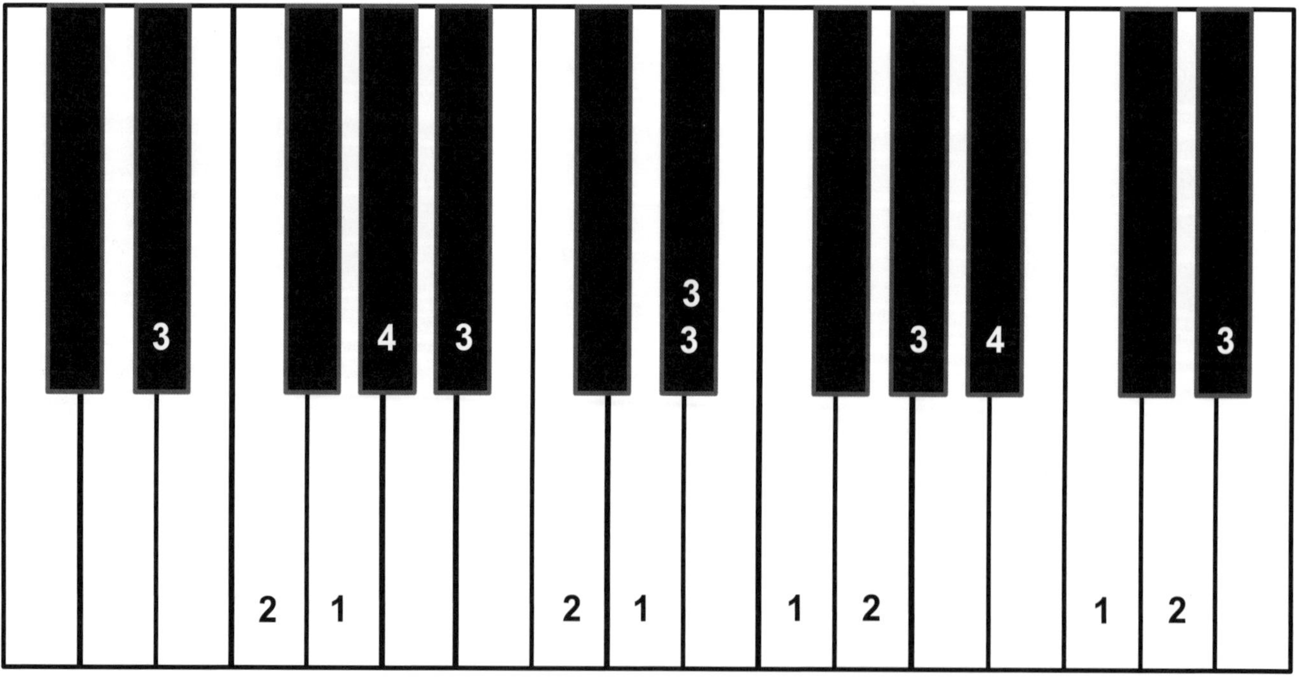

D Harmonic Minor
Contrary Motion Scale
PLAY THE CHORD

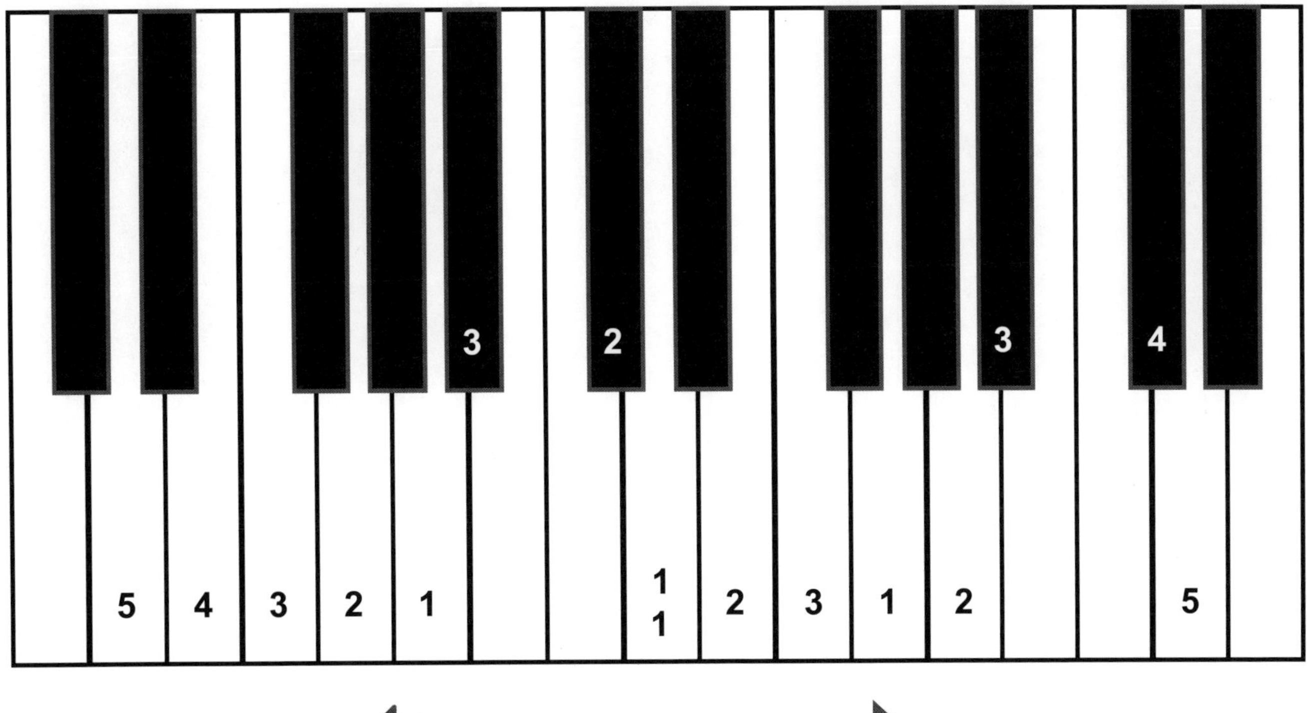

LH RH

C Harmonic Minor
Contrary Motion Scale
PLAY THE CHORD

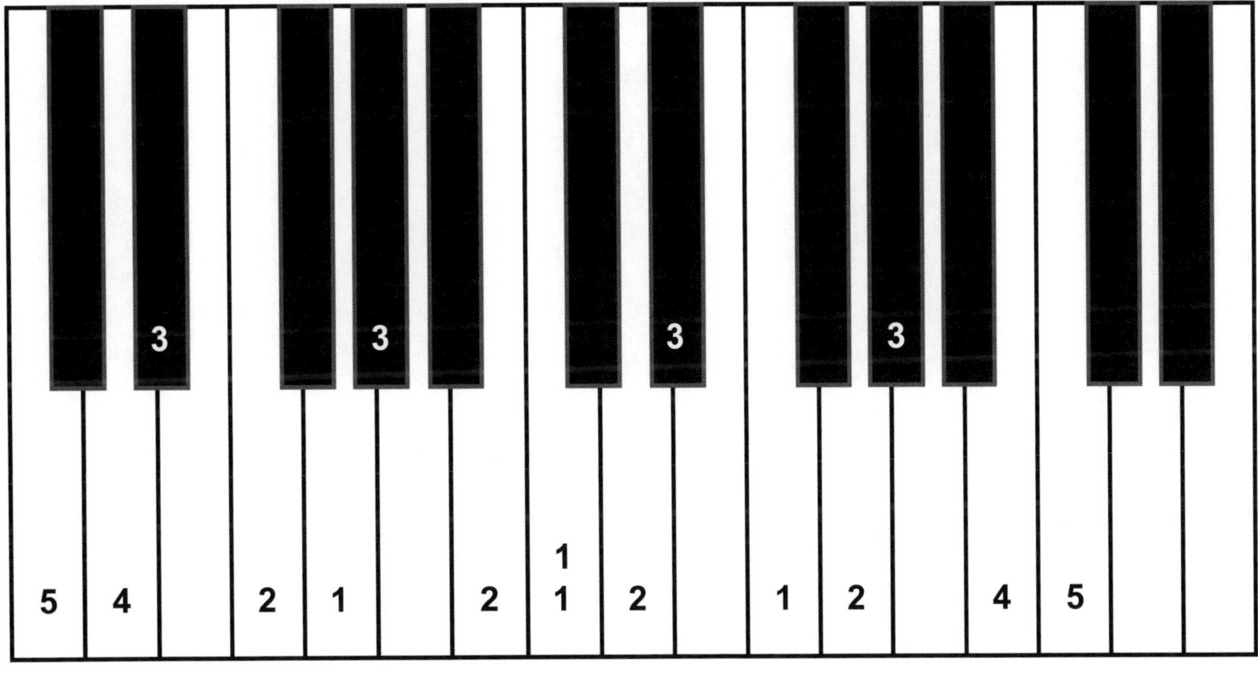

F Harmonic Minor
Contrary Motion Scale
PLAY THE CHORD

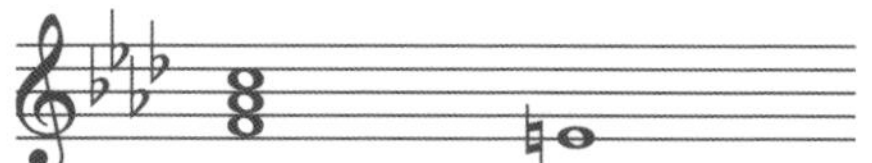

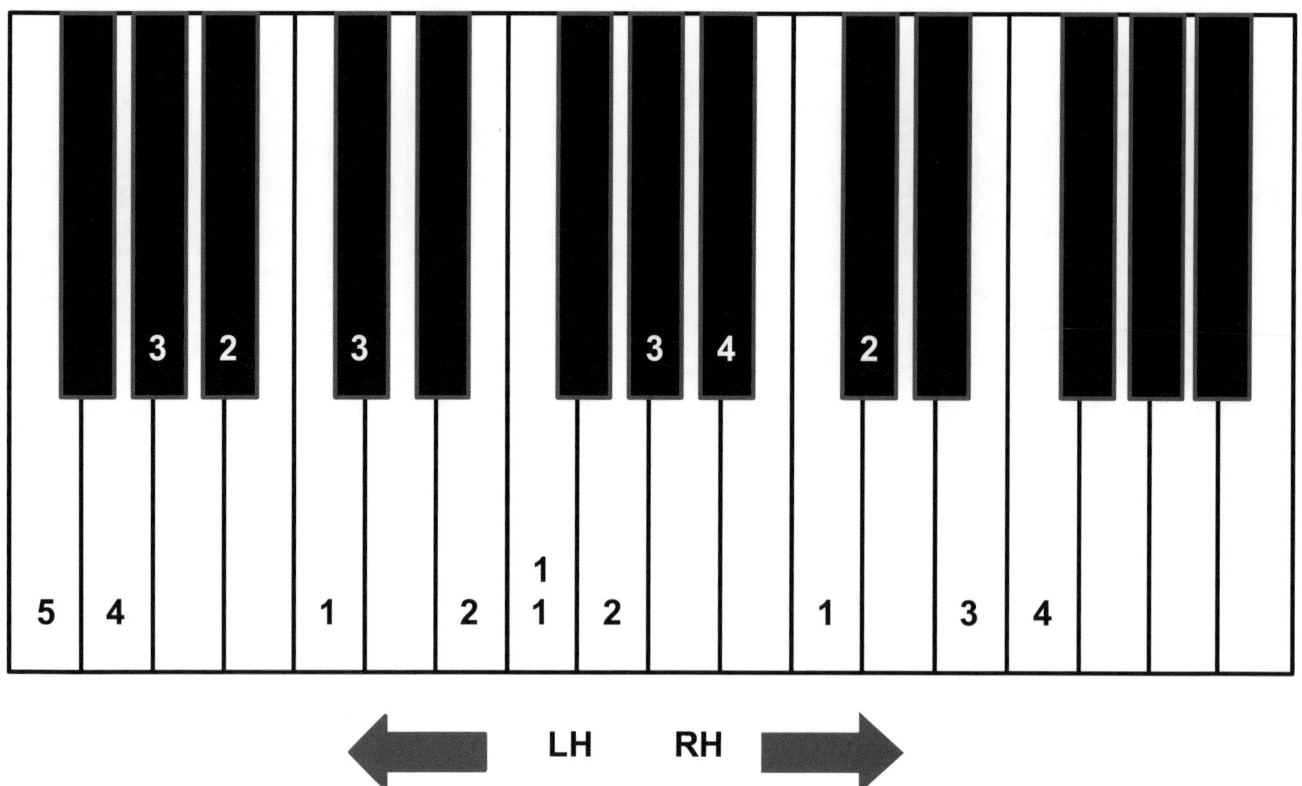

Db Major
Contrary Motion Scale
PLAY THE CHORD

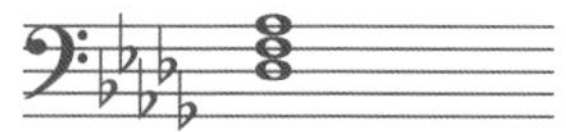

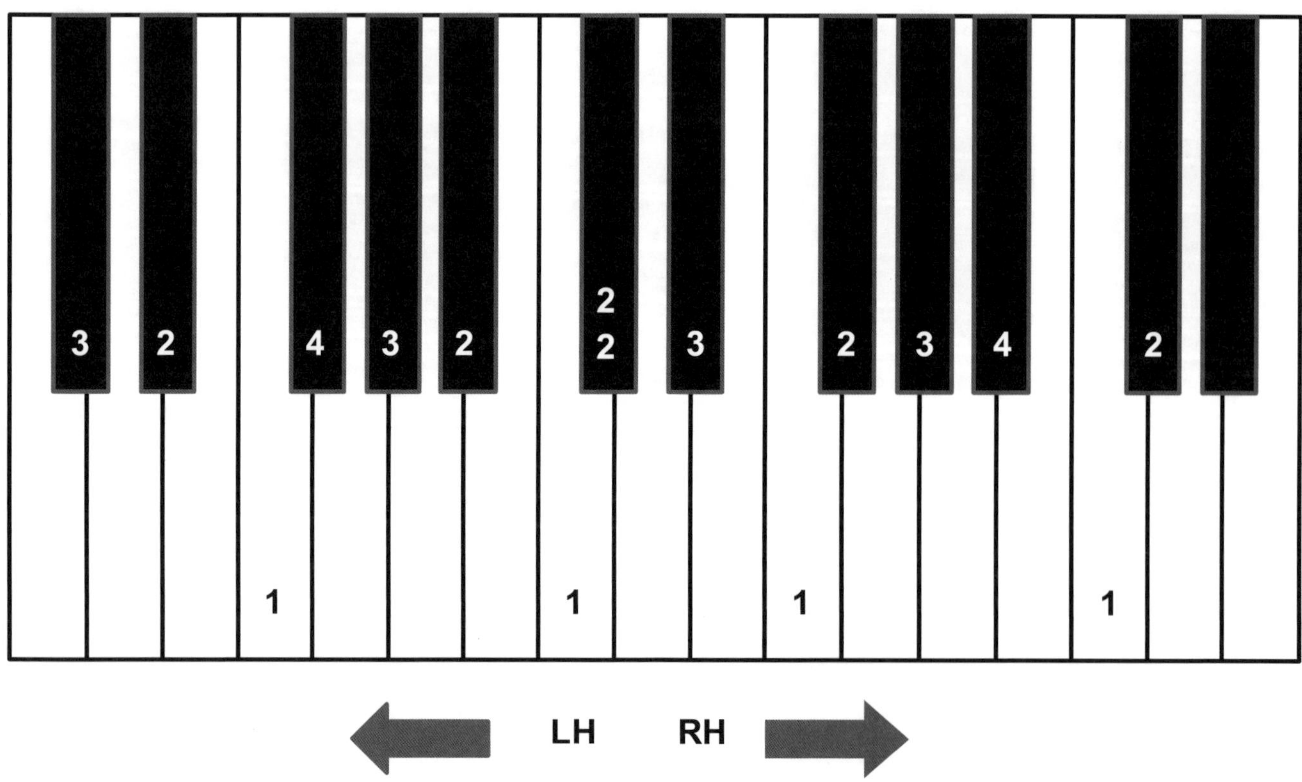

C# Harmonic Minor
Contrary Motion Scale
PLAY THE CHORD

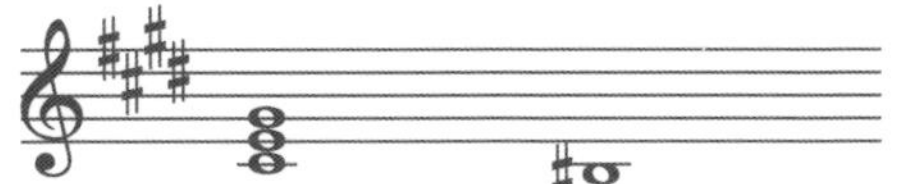

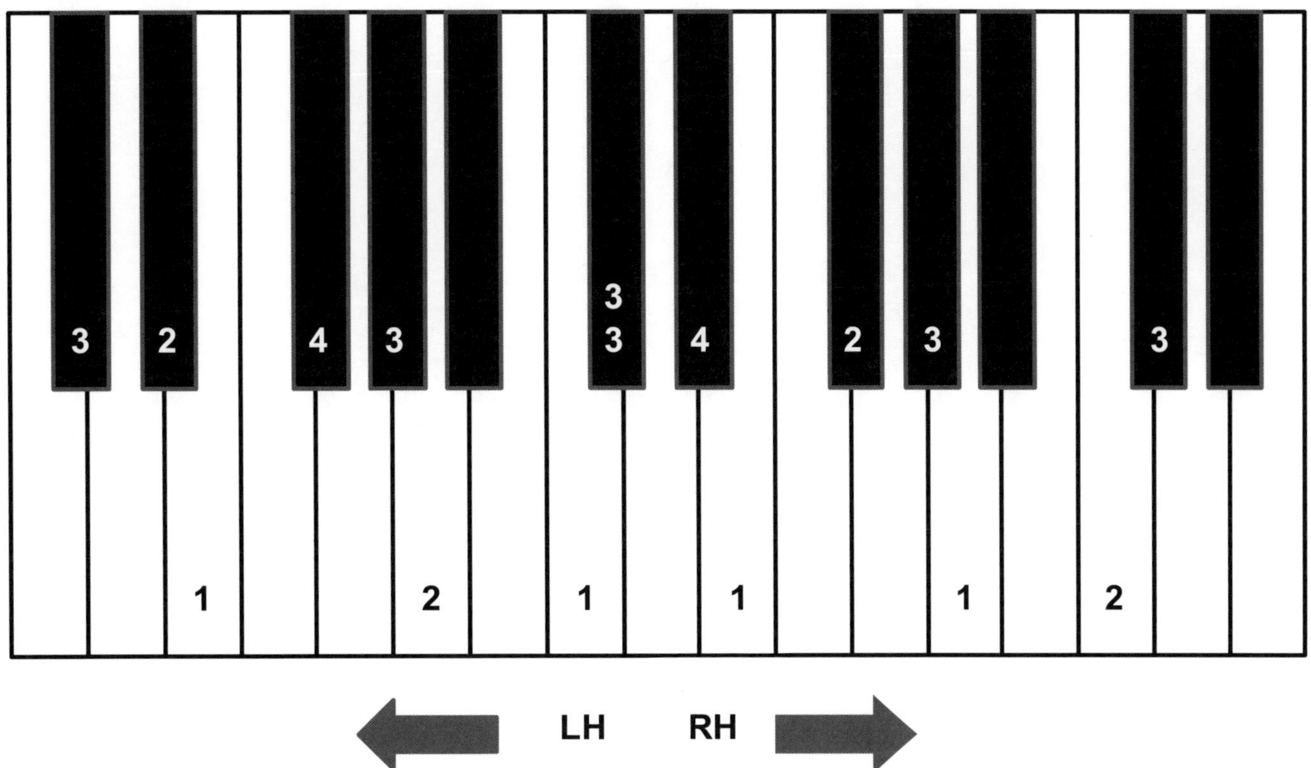